AUTHORITY AND ITS ENEMIES

AUTHORITY AND ITS ENEMIES

THOMAS MOLNAR

ARLINGTON HOUSE·PUBLISHERS
NEW ROCHELLE, NEW YORK

Manufactured in the United States of America

Library of Congress Cataloging in Publication Data

Molnar, Thomas Steven.
  Authority and its enemies.

  Includes index.
  1. Authority. 2. Liberty. I. Title.
JC571.M745   301.15'52   76-8506
ISBN 0-87000-340-2

Contents

1. On Authority   7
2. The Nature of Authority   15
3. Authority in the Life of Men   29
4. The Enemies of Authority   78
5. The Restoration of Authority   104
6. The Nature of the Restoration: Augustan or Despotic?   121
7. The Limits of Authority   131
    Index   139

1.
On Authority

Our ordinary experience in today's family, school, court, church, and nation is that authority—of father, teacher, judge, priest, and president—is hard to maintain, if, indeed, it has not actually broken down. Whose fault is it? Is authority undermined by identifiable people and forces—or is it simply not exercised? Some would point to the popular pedagogic theories of John Dewey—"democracy in the classroom," for example—as the culprit. Others, like the late Jean Cardinal Daniélou speaking about the causes of the church's turmoil, would say that authority does exist, it is there, but those who ought to exercise it hesitate doing so.

Almost two decades ago, sociologist David Riesman called our attention in his book *The Lonely Crowd* to a new type of man that he labeled "other-directed." Such a man, nurtured by our civilization at this point, has no strong convictions and beliefs; he receives anonymous orders from his social environment and social peers, conforms to them, obeys them mechanically. According to Riesman, this type is a changeover from the earlier American "inner-directed" man who knew what he wanted, made individual choices, and had the courage to defend them. Now a superficial observer may conclude from Riesman's study that the "other-directed" man is more conscious, rather than less, of the existence of authority, which he recognizes and to which he conforms. The truth is

7

different. The "inner-directed" man is aware of authority because he, too, exercises it. He knows his place in the hierarchy of society, his personality has clear contours, he makes decisions and receives decisions. All around him there are "inner-directed" men, exercising authority: father, teacher, pastor, family physician. When he accepts their authority, he copies firm attitudes which he learns to value and admire. He wants to be like they are. This shows that by its nature authority is *personal,* or, at least, it has personal ingredients even though it is not necessarily visible. We obey God not because we see him; great moral and political leaders do not have to be present—in fact they may be long dead—in order to be respected; tradition has authority over us because our forebears had set down its meaning and its structure. However, when the social situation is more restricted and its manifestations are more frequent, as in the family, the school, and in the maintenance of order in the street, authority must be concretely present in visible form. It is exercised regularly, perhaps even uninterruptedly, by parent, teacher, and policeman.

Is authority really needed in these smaller social spheres? The question is legitimate since we often hear and read statements that, except for very small children, every individual ought to be allowed freedom of expression and the right to decide what is best for him on all matters. This, at any rate, is the prevailing view; contradicting it may bring social penalties. A few years ago over the waves of a New York radio station I debated a lawyer who insisted that no authority (law) ought to curb dealers in pornographic literature in the display of their wares in shop windows. Also, recently, the ACLU proposed that primary school children should have the right to take their parents to court. A number of court cases ensued when long-haired pupils were ordered by principals or teachers to cut their hair.

These are samples taken from a vast number of situations where many of us feel that while freedom to act as we wish is a good thing, nevertheless *someone* ought to have the right to enforce a certain norm. Reflecting upon it, we soon find that this norm cannot in all cases be the outcome of a consensus or of a majority choice. Majorities are shifting, and what gives a norm its value (its *normative* character) is precisely that it is durable, not subject to popular whim or majority pressure. A norm is then a way of believing, speaking, or acting, which is consecrated by both reason and custom, one strengthening the other. And authority, if we base it on this formulation, appears as speech and action from the secure base of a norm. Otherwise, speech and action may be incidental, not binding beyond an immediate effect, or outright arbitrary, enforced but unreasonably.

After these somewhat abstract considerations, let us turn to the prob-

8

lem of the presence and absence of authority in situations where we experience the problem. Experience and reflection will tell us that there are natural groups and others which, while also natural, are better described as consequences of complex interactions between individuals and groups. I call the family a natural group—it is the basic social cell—and I call, for example, an art movement or a censorship bureau a complex social group. There are no societies without some form of the family—extended or simple—but many societies do not have artists associated according to devotion to a style, or censorship which deals with complicated matters of value and moral or political critique of existing norms.

The mere fact of speaking of families indicates that certain functions—permanent ones—are fulfilled by a group of people called father, mother (eventually grandparents), and children (eventually uncles, aunts, and cousins). The functions are relatively easy to list: protection, the creation of an intimate and warm environment, the regularity of habits, the acquisition of a language, a frame of reference supplying and reenforcing the identity of the members. These functions, which are so "natural" that we hardly perceive them, follow from biological and psychological necessities, and also from an added element which we can only call *love*. It is often argued that this latter is merely our awareness that the biological functions are performed in a manner that satisfies us. To argue thus is, however, a willed depreciation, a conscious impoverishment of an experience we all have and which cannot be, without violence done to it, reduced to anything else. Family love is as much *given* as its external, functional manifestations. The child and the parent do not dissociate, when giving or receiving the act of protection, care, respect, obedience, and authority, from the love which permeates those acts and is one with them.

Now my contention is that *authority* is analogous to love. Every act within the family is either a manifestation of authority (and corresponding obedience or refusal) or a manifestation of its absence. At first sight, love could be represented by a larger circle, authority by a smaller one inscribed in the first. Love is always present in the form of care, consideration, gifts, gestures, and so on, whereas authority needs a precise external sign, a regular reaffirmation, a direction. I once heard a father say how he envied his brother who merely had to signal to his teenage sons in order to silence them when he was talking with other adults. "My son would continue talking," he lamented in a resigned tone. The case of the two brothers displays similar situations and similar sentiments of parental love, but they are made dissimilar by the presence or absence of authority. It is not difficult to conclude that love is more effective (and mutually more satisfying) when accompanied by authority. The latter is indeed a way of channeling love; instead of a general and ubiquitous emotionalism,

9

love becomes structured, apportioned, is made directive, I would even say "educational" if the term had not been devalued as a part of the bureaucratic jargon. Anyway, love is formative and humanizing when coupled with authority; in combination, the two are the cement of the family structure.

A popular writer on family life and teenage psychology insists that authority ought not to be obvious because then it provokes rather than soothes the child's temper. One of his illustrations is a fourteen-year-old boy playing ball in the family living room and being reprimanded by his mother. The boy not only continues, he becomes impertinent and exasperates his mother, who, in turn, begins to shriek, then breaks down in a fit of sobs. The writer's advice is that the mother ought to have explained why she would not tolerate ball-playing in the apartment. If a family situation were a formula of physics or mechanical engineering, the adviser would be right: the best way to save energy and unnecessary expenditure (in this case, of tears and anger) would be a rational planning of each participant's place and movement, a set of preexisting formulas for do's and dont's. The living family is, however, not a mechanism with wound-up parts; there authority must be exercised and accepted in many instances without prior discussion, not mechanically but on the grounds of the function that each member has as a result of age, status, experience, and consciousness of the general welfare (common good).

With the last expression we have made an important step toward understanding the nature and role of authority. Society consists of individuals and groups, the one as important and fundamental as the other. Rousseau was dangerously wrong with the first statement of his work on "social contract," that "man is born free, yet we see him everywhere in chains." Man is born free as God's child, but neither as a member of nature nor of society, if freedom means self-creation, self-sustenance, and unlimited license to do as one pleases. Man's (rather already the child's) freedom, and with it his individuality, is circumscribed by the freedom and reality of the social group. Philosophers will forever debate which comes first, man or society, but we can safely assert that the problem is falsely formulated. Man cannot function outside society, and the latter does not exist without the individuals who compose it. Yes, one may object, but the individual can at least survive alone. Even this is questionable. We have never seen an *individual alone*. There are, to be sure, sporadic instances: Tarzan, the hermits, or a few Japanese soldiers who, after World War II, disappeared in the jungle of the Pacific islands rather than surrender to American troops. But if we take a more careful look, we realize that not even these individuals were ever alone and that it is impossible to say whether they sustained themselves by their own

10

efforts, outside the physical (animal) act of feeding and finding shelter. Tarzan, or whoever his prototype had been, was not a complete human being until he learned to speak; besides, prior to his encounter with other men, he had been nurtured by animals and was a member of *their* tribe; hermits carry their memories and skills, even their motivation to become hermits, from society to the solitude of the forest; and the Japanese soldier chose his lonely life on the grounds of a prior loyalty—to the Emperor—which continued to sustain him morally. The Thoreaus of the world owe to society the very formulation of their wish for utter privacy.

Authority, at its elementary level, is then the natural price that the individual pays for membership in society, without which he would not be an individual, let alone a protected and integrated one. By these terms I do not mean exclusively "defense against aggression," which is practically the only grounds on which social philosophers of a certain school justify the existence of society and state; I mean by integration and protection the fact that we learn society's language, mores, and traditions, without which we would be individuals physiologically, but not in the human sense, that is, infinitely rich in thought, modes of expression and articulation, with a sense of identity and belonging, with rather clear reflective choices, preferences, refusals, and aspirations. Thus if nature shapes our immediately given body, society fashions our reflective life, our ethical being, our tastes, our personality. And by "society," let us remember, we mean family, school, church, state—all the social articulations that one calls institutions.

None of them could exist without *authority.* Just as individual man is unimaginable without the social group membership which helps him become a fully conscious, challenged, and challenging person—in the same way each social group can only hold together if it is differentiated according to objectives, functions, and persistence in survival. We have seen that, in the last analysis, there can exist individuals not belonging to society, but that it is questionable whether (1) they are men and women in the full sense of these words, and whether (2) they can survive. Similarly, there can be societies not held together by authority. In such a case, however, they are (1) temporary and fragile groups, threatened by the canceling of the coexistence contract at any moment, and (2) unable to survive due to the permanent inner defiance of decision-making. One may argue here, too, that some families grant complete freedom to their members, that children are brought up permissively, and that husband and wife give each other sexual freedom to gratify their desires with any outsider of their choice. Or one may cite the latest examples of hippy communes and others, similarly modeled. Nevertheless, such families are held together by outside pressure, that is, by a degree of conformity to

11

social mores where defiance of it would meet ostracism and even the intervention of the law. In the last analysis, they, too, submit to society's authority—if not in regard to behavior inside the family, at least in regard to what society considers as its own minimum requirement of external adjustment. The same is the case with hippy communes: they last as long as the inner tensions do not disrupt them, or, simply, until a secessionist subgroup decides to set up its own commune.

In short, groups not structured, or only loosely structured, by internal authority, may survive if they are few in number in proportion to the groups within that society. They pose no threat to the concept of authority because the authority exercised all around them creates a network by which they, too, benefit. (Similarly, conscientious objectors and pacifists can act according to their convictions only because theirs is an infrequent occurrence. Society around them provides for its own, and for their protection. Should their number increase beyond a certain percentage, the whole society, now defenseless, would succumb to a determined enemy.)

Authority, then, does not define a social group—what defines it are its objectives, tradition, the quality, and loyalty of its members—but it is the chief instrument in all these respects and directions. Authority formulates, and when there is need for it, modifies the objectives, articulates and keeps alive tradition, and reminds the members of the loyalty they owe to the social group. For these reasons, we may distinguish between two types of authority: *charismatic* and *institutional.* The first is an unplanned exception, and in spite of its rareness, it strengthens the human material over which it is exercised; the second is the rule, the normal, the routine. Thus it is understandable that we are awed by the first and are tempted to regard the second as unjustified, saying that only such authority should be respected which "deserves" it, which is outstandingly good, just, spontaneously exercised, and accepted. Yet those who crave charismatic authority and scorn or would disobey institutional authority make a grievous mistake: an institution might be defined as the place where all members benefit by the authority that the best among them would have naturally. Let us take an illustration. The majority of teachers in a school, like people in any community situation, are average persons in terms of talent and inspiration to their students. We assume their pedagogic and cultural background as well as their goodwill to be more or less the same. One or a few of them excel and they are loved and obeyed: they have *charismatic,* or let us only say, natural authority. Should the majority of teachers not be obeyed on the grounds that they lack natural authority? The answer obviously is that obedience on the students' part ought to be equal to every teacher so that the institution's objectives, teaching and learning, might be carried out as regularly as possible. The average teacher with no commanding personality thus benefits by the institutionalization of authority. The exceptional teacher does not need it; the average teacher does. And in this forever imperfect world the average will always be far more numerous than the exceptional. The institution as such equalizes, and makes possible, a certain function—in a situation where a noninstitution, based on a few exceptional persons' ability to attract pupils, would have to remain a perhaps exhilarating but rare and precarious thing.

The same example could be shown to be valid in the family, too. A father and a mother are not always admirable figures, and a child may often envy a friend for the outstanding personal or acquired qualities of his parents. Should this inequality invalidate the less admirable parent's authority, even though in terms of sheer "performance" of his parental function he does not live up to the high standard set by the other? In consequence, even when authority operates at less than the ideal, less than the desirable level, its essence must remain firmly implanted in the given social group by its institutionalization. And institutionalization, in turn, is a signal to the members that the human condition is such that majorities are mediocre, in need of protection in their functions, thus benefiting by a standard established for less mediocre minorities. Again, take an example: a subway car in a big city and an aggressive person riding it among more silent and peaceable travelers. The ideal situation would be that all occupants of the car are equally robust, muscular, able to defend themselves against the eventual aggressor. This is obviously not the case; some are weak, and one actually has the beaten "victim" look on his face. Why does the aggressive man not attack him? There may be, of course, several reasons, but one is certainly the authority of the law, even if not represented by a policeman. One might say, again, that the strong—as in the previous example, the teacher with a personal authority —do not need the presence of authority, they possess sufficient strength to protect themselves. But most people *are* weak; their only protection is an authority watching over situations in which they are at a disadvantage. And, understandably, the strong, too, are often in situations of weakness; they, too, are protected by authority.

Consequently, the nature of authority is that it extends beyond the person who could or would directly exercise it. In this sense, authority resembles the law. The law, however, is promulgated in the name of all people of a given society, so that by definition it covers a wide and distinctly circumscribed social area. Authority, as distinct from the law, is exercised on bases different from sheer enforcement. Its essential nature is that it is *exercised* in what would otherwise be a social vacuum, and that it is *accepted* voluntarily. By "voluntary" I do not mean that those

13

who obey authority give the bearer of authority their explicit consent each time after a consultation; I mean, rather, that authority appeals to a number of motives in us, as varied as are the personal and social responses in general: loyalty, fear, prudence, regard for others, desire to imitate, corporate feeling, and so on. Thus while law coerces, authority addresses itself to a preexisting consent of heart, mind, habit, and respect; while we *behave* before the law even if our intentions (literally: "inner directions") contradict or oppose it, we *consent* to authority (we are of one sentiment with it), we agree with its demands upon us. Ultimately we do so because respect for authority is as natural a response of our whole person as are love, contentment, pity, or pride of achievement.

2.
The Nature of Authority

The first chapter gave several instances of authority and made it clear that authority is inseparable from the group. We may now proceed a step farther and suggest that no group can exist without authority, that groups are constituted and cemented by authority. This is true of groups formed by man's *biological* nature and functions, such as the family, as well as of *socially* created groups linked to such social functions as work, defense, sport activities, and others.[1] Consequently, the discussion about authority is, first of all, a discussion about what makes a group, an amalgam of individuals kept together and functioning in cooperation.

There are several elements which are responsible for the creation and duration of social groups: aspirations which may be reached only through common effort, the awareness of danger, partnership in enjoyment, professional interests, and so on. Cicero's statement in his work *De Republica* (I, 35, 39) seems to summarize them:

> What prompts men to unite is less their weakness than the innate need to be in their fellows' company. Man is not made to live in isolation, to wander about in solitude. His nature impels him, even when he has everything in abundance, to unite with other human beings.

Yet, this natural inclination is not yet sufficient to account for human communities; after all, animals move around also in herds, bees and ants live and work in "societies" where the individual is proverbially subordinated to the monolithic whole. Except within a very narrow—and unchanging—gauge, the dimension of freedom and individuality is obviously absent in the animal kingdom, so that we refer to their "socialization" as *instinctual*—over against what in man's social and political behavior we call *rational.* Human groups are certainly prompted also by what is animal (instinctual) in man, but more by what reason tells man to do. Even the new science of ethology, the representatives of which find many common characteristics between human and animal groups ("territorial defense" and "aggressiveness" being today the most talked-about), must admit that animals hardly move out of their standard groups—whereas man chooses, changes, improves, and in many other ways modifies the group (rather groups, in plural) to which he belongs and, more importantly in this respect, he creates.[2] What if not *reason* dictates to him these choices and changes and new associations, suggesting possibilities, articulating satisfaction and discontent, instilling the desire to break up the standardized and routine, and to constitute new ones?

Rationality is indeed the faculty which tells us in *what kind* of groups we should live and to what extent we ought to integrate ourselves with it so as to preserve a large part of our independence. At the same time, we are also aware through our reasoning faculty that the choice whether to live or not live as a social being is extremely narrow, in fact it is practically nonexistent. Man is a rational *and* a social being; the two are inseparable as, for example, the phenomenon of *language* proves: we could not think coherently if we had no words—socially created instruments— with which to formulate and articulate our thoughts even when we do not utter them, sound them. Or take another illustration of man as social-rational being. A man or woman may decide at a certain age—the age of reason—to live a celibate or a married life, but they do so in the full knowledge of the advantages and drawbacks of either course. It appears that regardless of the variations of cultural patterns and of the so-called life-styles, men and women generally opt for marriage, that is for the formalized group. In the 1920s the newly established communist regime in Russia included in its program the acceptance of, even the preference for, free love; yet within a few years this became the shunned exception and Soviet society (and legislation) returned to the "bourgeois-type" marriage.

The first step in "social rationality" (if I may coin such a term) is then the conscious choice of living with others; the second step is the realization that living with others must be organized, not left to chance, that is, to the possibility of an instant and uncontrolled dissolution of the group. Human societies differ from animal herds (and from what some utopian

16

writers regard as the ideal society) also in that the human individual tends to establish durable relationships at every level, whereas a dog or a fish may have a different mate every spring, a mother may lie with her sons, and so on. For animals, each new season may bring a redistribution of their group life (although the fact of living in groups does not change), and this indeed may appear worthy of imitation to humans also, particularly in their search for novelty in the sexual partner. But for human beings the organizational scope of social life is more permanent; in fact it tends to be nontemporal, that is, morally binding. This is, perhaps, the most important distinguishing trait between animal and human societies.

What does the *organization* of groups mean, what I just now called the second step? It means the ordering of the group's own structure, and the ordering of the groups themselves according to a hierarchical principle. Let us consider illustrations.

The decisive experience of being a member in a group is that everybody has functions to perform according to the communal objectives, although, as the last chapter will show, these are far from being the only functions. In a political party, for example, the members divide themselves from the beginning according to future roles: militants at the base, the more regular functionaries, the treasurers, secretaries, spokesmen, directors of propaganda, finally the formulators of the program, the decision makers, the leaders. What accounts for this division of functions? Ideally speaking, talent and competence; in reality, seniority, skill, connections, certain pertinent abilities, and the like.[3] They are attributes, deserved or usurped, justified or imposed, less naturally fitting the organization than, let us say, age and experience are which make father and mother more fit to run the family than the children are, but factual and accepted nevertheless. The man at the party base may grudge the leader his higher position, but meanwhile he remains within his own sphere— like the child who also thinks that he could better fulfill the paternal functions, yet accepts the functions devolved on him by his age and inexperience. True, the son one day becomes a father, and with luck, willpower, abilities, or ruthlessness the militant may one day supplant the party leader; but these individual changes do not affect the rungs in the organization, its permanently hierarchical division. Why not?

Because there is among human beings a rock bottom of inequality which acts as a differentiating principle. Thus any communal enterprise must be based on authority which implements this inequality, spontaneously when persons emerge as "natural leaders," or by imposition when, as in myriad cases, one enters a group with a set structure. We saw it in the case of a complex organization like a political party, but it is equally so in an industrial enterprise, an army, the State itself. It is true even in the simplest case, friendship between two individuals: in various

17

situations the natural authority of one is recognized by the other so that their action as a team becomes itself differentiated. Authority is the condition within which human groups exist, as it is also the condition of membership in a complex group in which the smaller component groups are individual parts. Authority presupposes hierarchy, and inversely, there can be no hierarchy without authority. Let us imagine one without the other. Authority—of parents, elders, priests, functional superiors—which is not leaning on a hierarchy already in existence can only be a unique case, the kind we now call *charismatic,* described in the first chapter as the authority of the naturally masterful, influential, respected teacher. He has authority, but the group he forms with his students is not a permanent group; it disintegrates the moment they part. The same thing would happen with another type of charismatic person, a great religious leader like St. Francis and St. Ignatius, if the people around them were not consolidated into an order after his death. On the sole grounds of a charismatic authority no society may arise, because orderly and permanent functions would depend entirely on the chance encounter between the unique individual and his ad hoc public. Only the exceptional teacher, father, policeman, foreman, boss, or sports trainer would be able to prompt a group to function as a group, that is, like a multiple individual, a moral person, an institution. The absence of that rare, individualized authority would signal the collapse of the enterprise.

On the other hand, a hierarchical arrangement without authority invested at each level exhausts itself and becomes ultimately leveled; it vanishes. This happens in the history of weak states, for example, usually at the penultimate phase before a revolution. Habit and inertia still provide a sufficient number of routine acts for the bureaucratic apparatus to function, but the occupants of power at every level realize how little and how hesitantly they are backed by the power immediately above theirs—until the moment when it becomes clear that the whole edifice is brittle. Then we see the emergence of what historian Crane Brinton calls an "illegal government," a counter-power confronting the official one, which syphons authority away from the latter. Such a case shows, incidentally, the limits of authority: it is not enough to hold authority in a kind of unconscious manner; the authority-holder must be aware of its significance, of its content, of its requirements. Authority held but not exercised is the main symptom of the sickness from which a group, a society, a state, inevitably withers because the hesitation and lethargy at the top become rapidly sensed at the lower echelons; mutual distrust arises among official authority-holders, no one dare execute the half-heartedly issued orders, people in position of decision-making begin looking to the "illegal government" for authoritative directives. It is then evident that authority is based on the conviction, first, that authority is a

18

positive thing, and, second, that the use of authority for a given purpose is the primary condition of carrying out the social objective.

Today, what we call the "crisis" of Western society is caused by the lack of understanding of these two components of authority. When and how do we take cognizance that authority exists? When it is exercised, in other words when a kind of stream passes at the source of which there is an *act of will* (essentially a political act) and at the other end an *act of compliance*. This is authority's "naked" form, not yet rational, not yet for a moral purpose. But whether this is brought about by a nontangible law or by the written or spoken word, the essence of authority is manifest. It is obvious that in our society this kind of act of will has been decisively weakened, because authority is not regarded as something positive by its holders. It is remarkable that our contemporaries subscribe to the evolutionary tenet of the animal origin of man as a matter of scientifically demonstrated fact, yet they reject the corollary that men, like apes, live in hierarchically organized communities, with authority following from seniority, force, ability, and other such sources. But, as said before, while among animals authority is derived (as suggested by the studies of Konrad Lorenz, Robert Ardrey, Jane Goodall, and others) from physiological and biological attributes such as physical force, age, dominant male status and so on, among rational men authority aims at the creation and preservation of a *good* (effective, progressive, value-inspired) community, hence it is invested in individuals and groups possessing moral attributes. This explains also the institutionalization of authority among men where moral attributes become values and are then made permanent, whereas physical attributes among animals are transitory and diminish with age. This fact implies that instead of the herd instinct which corrals animals together, man accepts consciously not only the advantages of living in community, but also the duties and sacrifices that go with it. The chief of these duties and sacrifices is the acceptance of authority, the limitations of one's freedom by the interconnected and interacting links of authority. If this were not so, unlimited freedom would break up the social ties, leading to the same frustration as the complete lack of freedom. In other words, man's basic nature sets limits to the psychological space within which he can adequately function, these limits being *freedom* and *authority*. When one of the two suddenly breaks down, the group itself responds with a loss of vital élan, and its members, for no tangible reason, lose their spiritual, moral, and finally their physical integrity.

This has happened innumerable times when a social system, organized around a certain form of authority, broke down under the impact of a sudden jolt. The nature of the jolt may be identified as the sudden passage from one authority to another in such a way that either no new authority comes into being or the new authority is insufficiently perceived. For

19

example, following the Spanish conquest of Mexico, the Aztecs, accustomed to fearing their princes and priests and spending their lives in dependence of idols and sacred practices, found themselves all of a sudden enrolled in the Christian system, which they did not understand. On the one hand, Ursula Lamb writes, the various Christian practices, particularly confession, brought them back into the habit of always consulting their idols and priests; on the other hand, they also became lax with sin. Asked why, the Indians said: "In former times, no one did his own will but what he was ordered to do; now the great liberty has done us harm, for we are obliged to fear and respect no one."[4] Similar phenomena are observable in the course of migrations, particularly on the individual level. Take Negro families moving from the South to Northern cities. The absence (or sporadic presence) of the father in the family is balanced in the South by the many traditional customs and social ties which act as an anonymous authority. The father's absence in the midst of the migrated family causes disaster because nothing is customary anymore in the new milieu. Almost the same observations might be made with regard to white immigrants from Europe: even when an entire family is transplanted and the exercise of parental authority is continuous, the plunge into an environment in which authority is more lax than it was in the old country, or is inadequately perceived, creates tension, conflict, and *anomie,* the absence of law.

Thus we come to understand yet another aspect of authority: it is exercised for the community's benefit insofar as the community understands its raison d'être. Authority is the expression of social reason, and it is supposed not only to preserve this rationality, this organization and articulation of the group in view of the latter's objectives, but its task is also to keep reminding the members of the group for what purposes they are members. Inevitably, there are groups pursuing evil objectives, and there is authority which forgets its own function of preserving and reminding. A gang of murderers or the totalitarian State fulfills no rational purpose, and it must coerce (threats and terror are also forms of coercion) its members to remain members, either by the promise of immediate gain or by brutal methods. (A contemporary example of the latter is the Berlin Wall.) Neither can be said to be rational and moral objectives, nor can membership in such cases be called morally binding. On the other hand, authority which is allowed to lapse in a rational community is also irrational and immoral since it jeopardizes the community's existence and encourages asocial, subversive elements at the expense of the community's security, freedom, and well-being.

Nature assumes the charge of exercising authority over animal herds through built-in instincts, themselves attached to physiological, seasonal,

20

or other changes. The rule over the herd of an African elephant, an American moose, an Alaskan bear, or a sea elephant in the Antarctic is challenged by younger males during the mating season until the ruler finally succumbs to one who then becomes the dominant individual in the herd. This is not a rational, consciously grasped change of authority—and hence, exercise of authority—but a change like that of the seasons: nature manipulates one of its parts. Nevertheless, many biologists, psychologists, anthropologists, and analysts of behavior (as well as the workers in the new sciences, ethology and sociobiology, like Edward O. Wilson and Eibl-Eibesfeld) hold that the same thing occurs among men, too, except that here the motivations—Wilson and others would call it the gamut of genetic-based behavior—are more numerous. Simply put, animals would have a narrower, humans a larger choice of motivations, both cases either genetically or environmentally determined. One ethologist, Anthony Storr, writes, for example, that competition in space exploration between Washington and Moscow is merely a "ritualized" continuation of the cold war—in the same manner as chimpanzees in Jane Goodall's account ritualize their aggressiveness instead of really attacking. Accordingly, what human beings would add to animal behavior—which becomes a kind of tacit norm—is the complexity of the field of action (in the above case: contest) and an accompanying rich ritualization and symbolization.[5] But these theories fail to take into account that the similarity between man and animal is superficial, since what makes mankind a distinct species has no equivalent in the animal kingdom: man's imagination, his effort at improvement, his knowledge of good and evil. Let us bear in mind, however, that these qualities, admirable marks of humanness as they are, would make of the human being a wild, incalculable, and unaccountable creature in a group not cemented by authority. We may adumbrate such a situation from the behavior of some medieval sects, as well as other more recent ones which recognize no structure or authority. The possibilities that imagination, together with the penchant for moral evil, presents to men, men fully exploit, thus turning the group into a tumultuous, unruly, and impermanent gathering, something incomparably worse than an animal herd whose members are watched over by nature, that is, by their self-limiting instincts and lack of imagination.

One may argue, as many indeed do, that precisely these superior faculties permit human beings to *internalize* what seems to them an exclusively external authority, so that they end up obeying themselves alone and rendering "external" authority superfluous. The thinkers who entertain this view consider authority as a humiliating agency, counteracting and repressing the individual's genuine desires and sacred freedom. We shall return to this question when we discuss the enemies of authority in the fourth chapter, but we might say here already that the issue is similar to

21

the one discussed previously, the case of the charismatic leader. The latter does not need to be integrated in an institutional nexus; he can impose discipline (our example was the classroom) by the radiation of his sheer personality or abilities alone. Correspondingly, there are also strong personalities able to submit to self-authority. The majority of men is not of this kind, they need a more or less high degree of integration with the communal attitudes and objectives, made known to them by a habit-forming reminder; they need authority to be exercised not inside but over them. Once again, this is not only a question of authority, of some vague abstraction floating above the community; it is a rational guarantee of order and structure outside of which most people cannot adequately function. This is, incidentally, not an "elitist" position, since it holds that individuals exercising authority over themselves are nonetheless subject to external authority like everybody else. There may be, indeed, a serious discrepancy between the objectives of such individuals (in the service of which they discipline themselves) and the communal objectives.

Let us look at two cases, the religious order and the Israeli kibbutz, for the elucidation of these matters. One may say that in the first case, the individual motivation to submit to (divine) authority is extremely high, and that in the second case the motivation to protect the new fatherland from enemy incursion is also unquestioned. In other words, authority, God's or nation's, is deeply internalized in each individual, monk or kibbutz member. Yet, perhaps in no other case is external authority more vigorously enforced than in monastery and kibbutz. Have we sufficiently reflected on the reasons why the monk's 24-hour routine of prayer, work, vigil, edifying reading, and so on, or the kibbutz member's 24-hour readiness to work and take up arms are more, *not* less demanding of authority than the daily existence of society's average member? The reason is that the more authority is internalized—the higher the individual motivation—the more the group member interprets his function as service, demanding sacrifices and integrating him with the very foundation of his community. A more than human wisdom seems to have presided at this arrangement; those in whom the social awareness and willingness to sacrifice is strongest also submit to the most intensive type of authority. This is also why army, police, fire brigade and hospital personnel, men and women of voluntary dedication, stand under, and welcome, strong external authority: it completes the self-discipline which, because of its very intensity, cannot be trusted alone and needs to be thoroughly integrated with society's cementing service network.

Authority is thus not a monolith, its face is varied, it acts with a higher or lower intensity and concentration. It can be said to be as varied as the orders and functions to which man belongs in a well-structured society. According to the above reflections, we find authority in its most concentrated form in those categories on whose function society believes its very existence rests: religious, military, legal. Minimally structured societies, like tribes, concentrate the greatest authority in the assembly of chiefs and elders without whom there would be no tribal, that is social, existence. At the other end of the spectrum, private clubs, for example, bear a very light authority because from the community's point of view their existence is either not indispensable or is interchangeable. As a consequence, authority is most expressive of the community's existence where its function is to preserve the structured essence of society, that is, the basic *inequality*.

Authority is in itself inequalitarian because, as a previously used image showed, it is like a stream issuing forth from an act of will (individual, collective, divine—direct or delegated) and ending in an act of obedience. Put in another way, authority expresses the first fundamentally unequal act, constitutive of society. It would be tempting at this point to suggest that behind the act of will there is always a superior talent, a greater competence, an admirable person, or even a better organizer of common enterprises. Professor Carl J. Friedrich is of the opinion that authority is the act of "gaining another's assent," which would mean that a person may exercise authority insofar as he has "the capacity for reasoned elaboration"—namely, we would add, the reasoned elaboration of a matter involving competence, so that the others accept it, comply with it. This is the essence of authority, according to Friedrich.[6] This view leaves aside, however, a number of other manifestations of authority and a number of other motives for compliance. Fact is, we do not obey only a "reasoned elaboration," we may not even give our full "assent" when we obey. True, Aristotle argues that the well-ordered State is the one in which inequality is voluntarily accepted—and voluntary acceptance presupposes reason that all men by their nature share. Let us again use illustrations to show how authority is actually based on reasoned acceptance, as Aristotle and Professor Friedrich have it, and that reason transcends the ordinary definition most people give it.

During World War II, Japanese kamikaze pilots accepted the greatest "inequality" imaginable, that of perishing with one hundred percent certainty following the sole command of their superiors, ultimately of the mikado whose authority was supreme as it incarnated the nation. Lest we believe that this is a case of some Far Eastern fanaticism, let us remember that the tradition of great navies—British, German, and others—used to demand that commanders go down with their ships, even outside war situations. Here again, a supreme inequality was accepted, a sacrifice which was presumably mitigated in the dying officer's mind by the satisfaction that through his act he belonged to a corps sharing a noble code of honor. A third example may be taken from the annals of the Spanish Civil

War when Colonel Moscardo, defending the Alcazar of Toledo, refused to surrender it to the enemy even when the latter threatened to execute the colonel's son, Luis, whom they were holding as hostage (July 23, 1936). The threat was carried out under the father's eyes, but the fort was not surrendered.

Are these acts of compliance with authority—that of the Japanese, British, Spanish, and other governments—reasonable? Or, put in another way, is it reasonable on the part of these states to demand the ultimate sacrifice? If we answer that the ultimate sacrifice is not that of life but of honor, we merely enlarge the question to read: is authority which commands honorable behavior reasonable? In any case, since not everybody is asked to undertake this kind of sacrifice, we deal here with the issue of inequality—which may be put into the framework of contemporary parlance as an economic issue: whether a certain part of the population should accept to "tighten its belt" for the sake of going through a difficult period from which other categories of the population suffer less?

From all these illustrations we obtain the conclusion that authority presents in a reasoned manner the inequality which exists in every community; we realize, of course, that reason is compatible with the fact that in the community there are many orders grouping individuals, many sets of codes (code of honor, professional code), many functions with widely differing importance, benefits, privileges, rights, and duties. Authority explains and justifies these differences, although in many cases this is not readily understood. An adolescent may not appreciate parental authority, seeing no reason in its exercise. "You must do it because I want you to!" is often the parent's exasperated reaction. Chances are, the adult will later understand what the adolescent was unable to see—or he saw it but refused to yield, partly from stubbornness of will, partly moved by the desire to test the firmness of parental authority.

Ultimately, people obey authority for any number of reasons, none of which contradicts the others, so that it is not difficult to grasp authority's nature. It would be futile to argue that authority is obeyed because it has coercion on its side; this is a truism since authority is always to some extent coercion, and at least in non-totalitarian societies, people generally obey coercion because they know that it is by and large rationally applied and that it can be codified by law. In other words, people want authority —they are even prepared to pay for it in terms of reckoning with coercion —because they want community, an ordered and structured one, a life according to reason. Only angels and wild beasts live outside community, and, indeed, when a human being leaves his community it is to become either the one or the other. Furthermore, when man wants to live in an orderly community this means he accepts inequality. Let us not, at this point, conjure up feudal abuses, slavery or serfdom, privileges before the

24

law, the economy weighted against a group; a reasonable society is structured according to the generalized principle of subsidiarity, which implies that in a society every group, from family to State, has distinct tasks it is best able to perform, and that these tasks are hierarchically organized for the sake of self-help and mutual help. In consequence, the social body is neither a haphazard juxtaposition of independent groups acting in self-interest, with a vaguely formulated government guaranteeing "law and order," nor a leviathan which crushes (disarticulates) the citizens and reduces them to an undifferentiated mass; it is a network of structured communities where, ordered to the common good, these communities occupy a certain place and a relative importance. Each in its own right may occupy a place and possess the corresponding authority; yet this authority can be exercised only because outside it and above it other groups exercise also the authority devolved upon them. It is useless to ask, as is often done nowadays in permissive societies, that the individual family, for example, should exercise moral authority when more powerful and prestigious institutions—courts, political bodies, churches, schools, armies—are in the throes of turmoil and moral collapse. The principle of subsidiarity requires that authority be evident in the highest spheres so as to justify and support the lower ones. This is precisely the condition for the lower ones to perform their primary functions. Thus authority is first of all public authority; as such, it transcends the private authority, yet it includes and preserves it.

In spite of all the crucial things that were said of authority—its foundation in inequality, its hierarchic character, its function of structuring the social body, its organization and expression of social reason—authority is not a mere political principle. It has roots which may be properly called mysterious. James I spoke of the "mystery of the State" derived from the king's "divine right," itself resting upon divine law. St. Paul said that all power (by which he meant legitimate authority) comes from God.

The mysterious character of authority can be, and has often been, interpreted excessively and described as a mystique of power, a cult organized around the holders of authority. This is not what we mean. The mystery is, so to speak, contained in the realization that social existence has its own foundations, reasoning capacity, and moral dimensions—just like individual existence, although society as such has neither "consciousness" nor "conscience." Society is not merely the sum of its individual parts, it is a reality in itself, with moral and spiritual dimensions. The discrepancy between our observation of individual (human and animal) and social selves, and the impossibility of reducing the data of the second to those of the first, make us speak, perhaps rightly, of a *mystery*. Everything social, in spite of its "de-mystification" through statistics,

25

polls, and computerization, has a mysterious aura about it, and most of all such phenomena as authority, hierarchy, and inequality, because they are obviously not parts of man's experience when he contemplates himself in isolation—which is the way we look at ourselves most of the time. Authority, hierarchy, and inequality transcend us, thus we tend to regard them as mysterious.

There is no reason to quarrel with this view, in fact it (the mystery of authority) is inseparably imbedded in the exercise of authority. Even the enemies of authority have recourse to authority in the very process of demystifying it or abolishing it.[7] Ethologists Konrad Lorenz and Robert Ardrey are, in a sense, also intent on reducing authority (and its "mysteries") when they argue that man is naturally inequalitarian since he belongs to the superior primates among whom conflict is natural for the first position in the herd. Lorenz shows that inequality is indispensable for the formation of groups, and Ardrey writes that group efficiency is in direct proportion to the strictness of hierarchy. Others (Erik Erikson, Helmut Schorr) argue, on the contrary, that authority can be eliminated (in family, army, factory) if the child, the soldier, the worker are enabled to identify themselves with the orders and instructions they receive.[8] True, a clear grasp of what authority is and how it functions requires that the fact of authority be understood with the help of reason. The error of Lorenz, Ardrey, and others is, precisely, that they derive authority from the genetically determined habits of superior primates, whereas in the human species we accept authority on rational grounds. (The least rational, that is, the child, rebels most). Yet, it does not follow that every manifestation of authority must be explained until reasoned consent (identification) on the part of the commanded and instructed is achieved. Once again, the soldier, the worker, and so on, comes easily to terms with the fact that a reasonable authority is exercised over him and does not demand a separate legitimation of authority each time it is exercised. This is so because at the other end of the process authority creates trust and a feeling of security without which orderly group functions—and individual functions—would break down to the detriment of the commanded person as well as to the detriment of the holder of authority. This point is brought out in H. J. Eysenck's critique of the Skinnerian presuppositions about a well-functioning society. Skinner holds that a system of rewards and punishments ("reinforcements" of desired behavior) may induce in human beings, just as in animals, the socially positive attitudes. An experiment was devised to test the hypothesis: two groups of children, differently brought up (traditionally and progressively) but both refusing to eat their spinach, were made to eat it, the first group by the old-fashioned authoritarian method, the second by rewards. The result was that both groups ate their spinach—but the children who acted under inducement stopped doing so when rewards were no longer forthcoming, whereas the traditionally brought up ones continued.[9] Eysenck does not say so, but it is evident that the latter had a better grasp of the total situation, that is, of the family environment, and decided that parental insistence, generally directed toward the common good of the family, may be good in this case, too. In other words, the person who accepts authority is not "stupid," "subservient," or "unimaginative," and the one who rejects it is not necessarily "bright," "innovative," or "courageous." Acceptance or rejection of authority is dictated by convictions rooted in a philosophy to which the above labels do not apply.

Notes

1. The distinction between "natural" and "social" is merely a concession to a prevailing jargon. "Social" is as "natural" as is natural itself. Institutions have their origin in human nature just like, according to natural law, the family and the State. This is a central truth, and if we ignore it, our discussion of authority is essentially vitiated.

2. Not only the ethologists (Ardrey, Lorenz, Tinbergen, Eibl-Eibesfeld, *et al.*), but the behaviorists and environmental determinists, too, (Margaret Mead, B. F. Skinner, Ashley Montagu, *et al.*) insist on basic and decisive similarities between animal and human groups.

3. The principle of articulation varies from one group to another. The more fundamental a social function is—army, church—the more regulated its principle of promotion. In less basic groups the members are more interchanged, which means that authority is more personal, less rigidly viewed. It is interesting to note that an industrial or business enterprise occupies a median position; the farther away we get in time from the early factories of the industrial revolution, the less authority we find, together with a more flexible promotion policy.

4. Ursula Lamb, "Religious Conflicts in the Conquest of Mexico," *Journal of the History of Ideas* XVII (1956), p. 4. [My italics.]

5. All animal researchers agree today that animals, too, engage in rituals, particularly in the courting period.

6. Carl J. Friedrich, *Tradition and Authority* (New York: Praeger, 1972), p. 55.

7. The par excellence antiauthority writer, Max Horkheimer (director of the famed Frankfurt School and coauthor of the study *The Authoritarian Personality,* New York: Harper, 1950) displayed a very authoritarian behavior vis-à-vis his disciple, Jurgen Habermas (present director of the Frankfurt School), who disagreed with him on various theoretical issues and who was obliged to take his diploma elsewhere than in Frankfurt. The central quest of Horkheimer was to discover the reasons for irrationality and destructiveness (by which he meant also "authoritarianism") still pervading the rationally organized industrial societies. But, as we said, authority *is* rational, and it must be, perhaps, more explicit in industrial than in archaic societies where it is supported by the whole social structure with its religious roots.

8. H. Schorr, "Eliminierung der Aggressivität?", *Politische Studien,* München (April 1975), p. 251.

9. "Behaviourism, Pro & Contra," *Encounter* (July 1975), p. 30.

3.
Authority in the Life
of Men

The principle of authority is one, but the objectives and articulations of authority vary according to the group whose structure it organizes: family, classroom, workshop, army, or indeed the State. These are occasions for different manifestations of authority, yet it is worth reflecting upon the fact that the exercise of various authorities within a society seem to be synchronized or in some other way linked to one another in a network. The collapse of authority within one institution, let us say the courts, is soon accompanied by the weakening of authority elsewhere: in church, family, army, and so on. This is an historically observable phenomenon, and our society is no exception. We may speculate on the reasons for it, but I think the most obvious answer is that society is an interlocked network, not only in the sense of the citizens' material dependence on each other, but also in the sense of their moral interdependence. Social life rests on a great deal of imitation—as is shown by the language we use, the fashions and fads we copy, the habits we assimilate—and *moral imitation* is one of its aspects. When someone does something unusual—good or bad—ripples seem to depart from him in all directions and others are affected by them. If a group of people becomes addicted to drugs, for example, this behavior immediately attracts attention: it induces some to imitate the original group, while it repels others. A widening sphere of

29

people become aware of the act and its moral implications, whether they react positively or negatively to it. Nobody remains insolated in a society, even if in most cases the reflections, attitudes, and responses represent waves too small for statisticians and pollsters to follow and study them. What is sure, however, is that innumerable influence waves crisscross in society at all times, and that the more powerful ones affect us all.

Now, one of the functions of authority is to act as a conserver of long-approved influence waves (or lines of behavior). Positivist social thinkers hold that authority cannot and should not go beyond this role: whatever society regards at any one time as positive, that is, within its best interest, is the supreme law that authority ought to serve. If a given society has cannibalism as part of its mores—or drug addiction, polygamy, the burial of members of the household with the dead master, slavery, and so on— there is no superior law to contradict, let alone abolish it. This view justifies the legalization of abortion in case a majority is found to approve it. The question is not answered, however, whether a parliamentary (congressional) majority may be called "popular majority" or "moral majority." It is certainly less than the unanimity of a tribe, for example, where cannibalism has been practiced from time immemorial by all members as part of a religious ritual.

To other than positivist thinkers it appears that society is not the final judge in these matters, and that there is a moral authority transcending society which ought to be consulted. Indeed, when the first sign of a spreading habit of drug addiction comes to our notice, we do not wait for the law, or medical opinion, or social consensus to make statements about it, our *moral intelligence* tells us that it is a condemnable act. Later we find, of course, that social consensus is in agreement, discounting some nuances, with moral intelligence, and that the law follows soon after, so as to complete the tripartite source from which authority generally flows. Consequently, it is not hard to see that authority, as it comes to be exercised at various levels of society, is not an arbitrary act, something that is often described as an "authoritarian" act, but one in conformity with social judgment and mores *and* with man's naturally moral thinking on the matter. It is thus understandable that authority's manifestations in family, church, factory, and elsewhere follow the same pattern and are inspired by the same content; the distinguishing factors are the specific character of the group and its objectives. There are groups in society because there is a variety of objectives which conform to individual aspirations as well as to communal functions. Thus every institution embodies two profound strains, one individual, one communal, hence its stability and its presence, with modifications according to time and geography, in all societies. Let us analyze in the following pages the function of authority in a number of institutions whose universality cannot be denied.

(a) Authority in the Family

It may be good to recapitulate here the three main features of authority we have implicitly distinguished in the preliminary discussion. The *first* feature is that man, lacking the sure-footedness of animal instinct, needs social enforcements enabling him to conform to his very nature as a social being. Authority, in this sense, does not actually define for him the common good or the partial good, but it does point the way toward it and provides a considerable stimulus for its attainment. The content of authority's command does not have to be made very precise at this point; it is sufficient for it to provide a direction, a *Do* and a *Do not*, to act already as a source of behavior. The *second* feature is that authority structures the fundamental inequalities among human beings, and in this respect it extends the benefits enjoyed *naturally* by the best to all members of the group. Our earlier illustration was the classroom and its discipline, which is not matter-of-factly enforceable by the majority of the teachers; authority is the means of ensuring that a seemingly homogeneous multitude divides into permanent strata and thus performs a certain number of ordered tasks among which there is a hierarchy of importance. The *third* feature is that authority, which was only a pointer in the first formulation, contains at least some concretization of the common (or partial) good, inasmuch as it is based on moral insight reinforced by social consensus in its widest sense. All this does not mean that the use of authority automatically leads either to virtue or to the desirable social behavior; but it supplies an indispensable persuasion as it possesses sanctions in cases where reason does not suffice.

Although the family is always called the basic building block of society, it is at the same time the most ambiguous, together with the State, of all institutions. Of all authorities, the paternal is least protected by the law and by a growing custom, perhaps because it is assumed that it rests anyway on solid biological foundations. This was not always the case. In Rome, the *patria potestas* was an awesome institution, allowing the father the right of life and death over his children, including their exposure after birth if found deficient or malformed. In many archaic societies the equivalents of Roman paternal rights have always been maintained, and up to the Eighteenth Century in France it was an accepted custom that fathers dissatisfied with their sons' behavior (such as squandering the family fortune) could petition the king for the issuance of a lettre de cachet, locking up said sons in the Bastille. Yet, the intimate, self-sufficient character of the family does not allow a very close observance of these laws. What has remained of them in modern jurisprudence is paternal responsibility until the age of majority, plus such rights as, for example, the choice (increasingly theoretical) of the kind of instruction the child should receive. But for several reasons, financial, geographical, legal (busing, for example), this parental right is slowly being eroded, and government increasingly determines the child's upbringing and education.

Authority, as we have seen, is not only legal, it is primarily moral, rational, and habitual (both uninterrupted and habit-forming), and at all times it is rooted in its counterpart, the innate desire to respect authority. The child is born *into* a family, and by the time he begins to reason and to make his feelings a conscious part of his existence, he has developed habits, chief of which is his acceptance of his parents as sources of authority. Up until this age the use of authority is biologically, psychologically, and morally vital, the child could not have remained alive and grown without it. The difficulty arises when groups other than his family begin to compete for the child's loyalty and acceptance of parental authority: friends, other families, later school, together with other institutions and the general tonus of the environment. Since parental authority is inseparable from love, the good of the child is easily perceived by the parents as a case for special consideration, namely lifting the child above the rest of the environment, hence "spoiling" him for society. Such a use of parental authority is misguided, because it is unreasonable and destructive of other social authorities to which the child is or will be subject. On the other hand, the opposite situation may also exist; in fact, today it is the more frequent and the more dangerous one: when the highest social institution, the State, passes and enforces laws lifting the child from under parental authority, such as imposing on schools curricula detrimental to family life and parental authority. Sex education is one such instance in this country; legislation in France concerning the use of contraceptives without parental approval by girls fourteen years of age is another. I saw in Italy the most excessive and shocking case to which the logic of the counter-parental interference may lead: privately sponsored posters on streets inviting children *(bambini)* not to tolerate coddling by parents who "only call them good and nice the better to exploit them"! In all these cases either the State interferes with the family's rights or in its extreme permissiveness it tolerates interference by private agencies. The consequences are the same.

For this state of affairs the State alone is not to be blamed; responsibility is shared by trends and movements which are destructive of the family and to which the family members are increasingly tempted to make concessions. One such trend is represented by the women liberationists who undermine the family's integrity by referring to the necessary emancipation of women from such chores as making the beds and cooking the meals. The argument is based on the dissociation of the woman and her natural functions, or as one writer puts it, "lifting her from the condition of a woman to that of a human being."[1] The result is the drop of natality in a number of countries and the further efforts to reduce the birthrate to zero. There are cases when mothers with three children are abused by strangers on the street as if they were criminals for giving birth to more than the prescribed ideal of 2.2, allegedly sufficient to renew the population.

The other trend is to relegate parental authority to other institutions, and ultimately to the State. This happens, according to Marcel De Corte, when instead of subordinating the child to the common good of the family, the latter gives the child a privileged treatment, trying to secure his or her future in such a way that the family itself cannot cover the expenses and efforts involved. Inevitably then, the State rises behind the child as his increasingly influential provider and tutor, but in payment for its services, the State exacts the price of conformity to its interests and its philosophy.[2]

Thus the family authority which is permanently used (since the family is the number one and decisive civilizing agent of all human beings) faces two major challenges: one from inside, by which the child runs the risk of not being prepared for civilized life, and the other from outside, through legal intervention, which sets the child against the family and against the moral life that is the family's task to provide. These two dangers indicate the guideposts for the use of authority in the family; they tell the story with all the clarity required: the family must protect itself against two kinds of permissiveness, one which is the natural temptation for parents, the consequence of which is the spoiled child; the other is derived from social pressures, ultimately from bad laws, which encourage the child's lower instincts. Authority's task is to resist both, since one as well as the other lead to a warped, uncivilized, asocial human being. Usually, permissive education is blamed for disrupting family life, but not much is said about its disruptive influence on society, since John Dewey's avowed goal was to make democracy "work better." Yet, as the essence of permissiveness is the denial of authority (in fact, its shift to those who rationally ought to submit to authority), it also implicitly denies the concept of the common good. In other words, the partisans of permissiveness so completely trust the goodness of human nature that they believe that noninterference with the child's ways will automatically lead to good results. If we follow their logic, we find at the end a completely new society—or rather a "dis-society"—at every generation or even at shorter intervals, since every child permissively brought up follows his own will, views, and norms, and they are by definition not transferred to the next. Thus, the consequence of permissiveness, if it were allowed free course, would be the extinction of society, in truth, anarchy.

It has been suggested by the German ethologist Konrad Lorenz, among others, that certain permissive methods and schools are not so permissive, after all. The recently famous Summerhill is supposed to

33

enforce authority, but in devious ways, so to speak, so that the child is not aware of following in actuality the models (his teachers) whom he admires. Is this view not based, however, on a misunderstanding of the nature of authority? In an age like ours which fears, and scoffs at, authority, it is very unpopular to declare that the human being needs authority the way he needs love, friendship, togetherness, and other "outlets."[3] If we could make a chart of fundamental needs as we make an anatomical chart, the place for authority would not be difficult to locate; it would be near the center. To argue that authority, insofar as it is needed at all, must come dissimulated and "packaged" is the equivalent of holding that love, too, must be hidden as something shameful. In the case of America, it is very likely that we are now witnessing the shift of the puritanical mentality from one extreme to another: once, the show of emotions, even their existence, was a cause of embarrassment, and authority was the desirable attitude; today authority is condemned, and free self-expression is eulogized. If Summerhill and other similar methods persist in making authority "palatable" for the child, then one of two things occurs: either the child remains shortchanged in his very real need of complying with authority, or he sees through the mask of his teachers and parents, and remains contemptuous of authority in whatever form he will later encounter it. Both reactions deny his social nature.

(b) Authority in the School

Its rational nature demands that authority be first of all articulated according to the objective it pursues. Parental authority is permeated by love and gives the child solid emotional foundations which at the same time automatically justify in the child's own mind the use of authority. The farther removed we are, on the scale of the subsidiarity principle, from the intimacy of the smallest group, the family, the less love and authority will interpenetrate. At the peak of the social edifice, the State does not love the citizens, it uses authority as the essence of the governing function. One of the basic experiences of adolescent and later years as one moves away from the family circle into school, boy scouts, army, adult life, and work, is that with each new phase the stuff of life becomes more compact and serious, that one is less and less protected, that finally matters become a question of life and death, or at least of success and failure with all the consequences of the one or of the other. At each of these phases the goal of authority, hence its mode of exercise, too, is different. In school, authority must be essentially used for the preparation of moral and intellectual conditions for learning and learning itself, that is, the enlargement of the child's horizon in the direction of nature and of the past and present of his society: community, country, civilization.

34

Normally, the school is the place where the child is first introduced to sustained, systematic, and purposeful mental effort. Thus instead of *love*, authority is permeated here by the need to instill into the child the admirative grasp for the objects of his studies, an admiration which elicits from him a continuous effort. Philosophy is born, Aristotle held, out of man's faculty to marvel at things (*thaumadzein*); not just things he perceives with his senses, we may add, but also concepts, lines of reasoning, the concatenation of phenomena in nature and in the mind. Among these objects figures man's place in society as well as his freedom from society, an endlessly challenging subject about which every man forms his opinion, taught to him throughout his life by his own experience. In short, this gradually opening vista for the understanding of which the child can be only slowly prepared requires *respect* on his part, respect for what he learns and for those imparting him the knowledge. This involves quite a big step away from the family atmosphere of love and authority, because in the family the child's habits solidify very gradually and at the beginning unconsciously. When he enters school, learning and respect for learning must be instilled in the already conscious young being who naturally resists the formation of new and painful habits. Without authority, in this case based on respect rather than on love, the teacher cannot perform his task, which is a big step forward in the civilizing process. It is also a notably difficult task since the process of teaching and learning, unlike the ordinary family processes, takes place between "strangers," teacher and pupil. The former's authority must be moral as well as intellectual, because the child perceives him surrounded by the aura of marvel which the new things learned cast on the teacher. He stands before the child as the representative of the totality of the outside world, as someone responsible for the outside world. This is an eminently moral situation, in fact, at the beginning more moral than intellectual. [4]

There is more. In the child's world the figures of parents and teachers stand out as all-powerful organizers and arbiters of life with its many as yet incomprehensible situations. This attitude is profoundly human, and later in life the adult continues to have admirable figures, larger than life-size, on his horizon. [5] When he turns "cynical" and professes contempt for everything and everybody, he pays involuntary tribute to the admirable figures whom he did not find or failed to recognize. But respect cannot be forcibly elicited; it is something spontaneous, at least for the child. The school is then also a place where respect is socialized, extended to an entire community—the teachers—including those not deserving it or unable to elicit it through their personal qualities. It is in school that we learn that respect is due not only to the respectable, if one may put it that way, but to whole categories because of the function they collectively perform. [6] To achieve this, a large amount of authority is needed, since the child's moral chemistry does not make him a spontaneous respecter of classes of people, outside his parents to whom his allegiance is based on preconscious experience and the unmediated experience of love. The teacher, on the other hand, merely mediates knowledge to the pupil, and unless he is a respectable person on other grounds, too, the pupil will not bring him his loyalty. Authority provides the bridge on which they meet and on which the child meets entire classes of society as well as society itself.

Does this mean that one inculcates hypocrisy in the young when he is made to respect whole categories of people instead of those individuals who deserve respect, or when he is taught manners that he must use in all circumstances? Manners and manifestations of social respect are not equivalents of hypocrisy, just as ethical commands do not discriminate between those toward whom one ought to be charitable and others toward whom one does not have to be. There would be no social coexistence without treating individuals *also* as members of groups, uniformly. We cannot tell merit from lack of it in normal social relations; we must hence give the benefit of doubt to something that stands above the individual (from the collective point of view), namely the function, the rank, the role, the representativity. We pay our respects to the *persona* which was the mask that the characters wore in Greek tragedies and which represented types, not individuals. Old age ought to be respected (to cite one example among many), even though not every old man or woman is individually worthy of respect.

In the course of these analyses we meet again the various opponents of authority. The classroom ought to be a "small replica of our democratic society," wrote John Dewey, and, paralleling his thoughts, his disciples and other thinkers have been trying to equalize the status of teachers and pupils (professors and students). No doubt this can be done, but only at the cost of undermining the school's implicit objective, education, instruction. All those who propose the classroom as an experimental station, a laboratory for better social relationships or political arrangements, interfere with and corrupt the school's primary function, teaching. This is not meant as a rigid rejection of change and reform; bona fide historians of education recognize the many changes—of curriculum, method, administration, and so on—in the course of centuries. But the core, namely the teaching of tradition-consecrated as well as newly important courses, has been permanently present and far more essential than an endless effort at rearranging the respective status of teachers and learners.

It is not surprising to find in the center of these controversies the problem of authority. It was also the axis around which the uprising in universities occurred in the years 1968–70. Let us note the main issue and the consequences of those years of turmoil in high schools and universities. It is not the ideological content which makes them stand out in the academic annals, it is the change of status, the attempt to take authority from the hands of teachers and to place it in the hands of students. Put this way, the statement is not quite accurate because the status shift benefited not only students but also, perhaps even primarily, the young professors, adjuncts, and assistants. This phenomenon then followed the course of all revolutions: the populace (in this case, the students) are the "raw material" of the assault, yet the power-eager class of people profit by it who are inside the coveted citadel but not yet masters of it. The result is that the status shift has put the lower echelons in power, in the name of youth cult, student power, historical revisionism, and what have you.[7] With this, the universities have ceased performing their function: the preparation, in a suitably scholarly atmosphere, of an intellectual elite. The nature of authority would dictate that such a task must be entrusted to an already existing elite, in this case the community of scholars, who elicit, in their field of activity, the same natural respect as fathers, elders, judges, and heads of state do.[8] The issue thus turns back to the structuring role of authority, more specifically to the structuring of inequality that can be particularly well understood in this context. Inequality in the case of schools and universities is undeniable between the level of knowledge of professors and students. The imparting of knowledge inevitably creates further inequalities due to the variety of student response, but authority also provides stimulants for higher attainment.

This observation may carry us a bit further toward the understanding of authority. The area of teaching may prove particularly apt for this purpose. It is often suggested—more and more frequently since the student revolt of 1968, that schools ought to be "pluralistic" and pursue as many and as varied interests as there are students with their particular wishes. In California a school district recently entertained the proposal that traditional courses be abolished (one wonders how many have been taught anyway in the last thirty years or so) and altogether new ones—life-, leisure-, and career-oriented—be introduced, among them such courses for credit as bicycling, hiking, canoeing, time spent in newspaper offices, electoral campaigns, traffic surveys, and so forth. The proposal was presented in the usual jargon about the happiness of the individual, the right of children to make decisions independently of their parents, the school and the curriculum finally placed in the hands of the real consumers, namely the pupils.[9] We have in this proposal both the ignorant rejection of what schools, by their nature, ought to teach, and the same kind of authority shift we noted in the whole tenor of the student revolution: away from parents and scholars, authority to the young themselves. Both demands deny the school's objective, so that authority, which is always in the service of the essential objective, is also denied. The term *demagogy* comes to mind, the intention to persuade people to act contrary to their rational human nature.

Projects destructive to institutional objectives, thus of authority, too, come also from more unexpected sources. A recent formulation of educational objectives by the Jesuit Secondary Education Association (JSEA) has this to say as "Number One":

> The primary educational aim of the Jesuit is the humanistic formation of students . . . . The human growth of students and of the faculty as well is of greater concern than the things being taught and learned . . . . We cannot . . . expect to be able to convey to our students any systematic comprehension of human nature or of the world through philosophical insight, ethical judgment, or theological reflection . . . . The perfect education today will transmit the basic skills of technology . . . . In a certain sense, today's *eloquentia perfecta* is possessed by that man who is value-conscious [how can he be if the Jesuits admit that the student cannot be taught any systematic comprehension of human nature and the world?], skilled, communicating and a technocrat.

In the spirit of this program, the school would become an adjunct of technology—although in their "Preamble to the Constitution of the JSEA," the Jesuit educators castigate the "old school" for accepting "the false values, warped assumptions, and class or cultural mythologies . . . of mainstream America," the false patriotism of the rich. The disturbing thing in these and other passages is not only that the Jesuit educators turn their back on theology, philosophy, and ethics, but also that they subscribe to the relativistic—and Marxist—assumptions that each new epoch has its own truth which negates the truth of yesteryear. This is no mere correction in the course of institutional objectives, it is the pulverization of authority which no longer cautions a rational choice. At one and the same time it undermines parental authority and, in fact, all authority exercised over the young. In *The New Totalitarians,* Robert Huntford quotes Swedish Minister of Education Carlsson:

> The new school's objective is to destroy respect for authority and to put in the latter's place the child's readiness to cooperate with the group. The old social order is breaking down anyway, we must find a replacement. As a result, we demand a collectivist attitude and we fashion the schools according to experience gained in labor unions.

Comments Huntford:

> When the Swedes destroy authority in the child's eyes, they mean the authority of parents, teachers and employers, not all authority. They condition the child towards perfect conformism, the acceptance of group-imposed objectives and methods. The result may well be, even if this was not the original design, that those who are in leadership position in Swedish society will have servile individuals at their disposal.

38

(c) Authority in the Church

All religions claim a divine origin and therefore a divine authority, both at their origin and in continuous action in the life of the faithful, that is, providence. One may even say that religious (divine) authority is the prototype of all authority, because the inequality and hierarchical character that all authority entails is primarily realized in that of God over men. This was true in every society, from the Peruvian Inca to the mikado's Japan where the emperor, king, or pharaoh was regarded either as god or as god's offspring, to the Western nations which accepted the divine right of kings. The French historian Marc Bloch wrote a large book about the miracle-making (*thaumaturgos*) faculty of French kings whose power of healing was attested to by generations. Bloch argued that the notion of healing power was derived from ancient Israel and proceeded, through Christ, to the kings of France.

When discussing authority in the church in such a book as this, we cannot take divine authority itself for our subject; we must proceed at once to divine authority as mediated by an institution, the church, which brings it in contact with human beings. What is the objective of this authority? All religions answer that the objective is *salvation,* in other words, the adherence to beliefs and acts which open for men the road to beatitude, immortality, and oneness with God's design. This supernatural objective enhances the church's authority above all other authorities since the objective now is not merely social integration according to man's rational nature, but his spiritual integration through faith, and also divine grace. There is here a higher level than society, beyond the expected and normally secured cooperation of various institutions. The cooperator with the human effort is not now parent, teacher, judge, but God whose will cannot be calculated, taken for granted, forced. At this point, the church's role becomes evident: it is the one authority which assists man's integration with the economy of salvation, although it cannot do more than the father or the teacher, namely bring within the scope of its authority the forever recalcitrant individual.

If the church's authority were exercised in proportion to the importance of salvation, it would be limitless, and thus tyrannical. We have seen, however, that every type of authority carries within itself a limiting factor in conformity with its rationality: in the case of the family, love stands in the way of the parent's harsh authority, and in the case of the school, the respect for the potential scholar (or simply, educated man) prevents the teacher from becoming a despot. In the spiritual community the supernatural respect for a God-created soul is the inhibiting factor or rather the factor which enjoins the members of the church, including the hierarchical superiors, not to treat each other according to worldly likes and dislikes, but in the light of the recognition that the *other*, too, bears the divine seal.

Religious authority is, consequently, as articulated as any other authority; it is exercised within limits, it recognizes its mediating function. In fact, this function is best perceived in the case of religion where the field of force between God and man, the two poles of mediation, is a kind of model for other types of authority also. The school mediates between outstanding cultural and scientific facts, on the one hand, and, on the other, the young waiting for integration with the world loosely described as the world of education and knowledge. The name of this mediation is teaching. The church mediates between God's will and man's aspiration to reach Him and meanwhile to obey Him and His commandments, an imperfect way of reaching Him while in this life. This is the meaning of the word *religio* (to link, to connect, to tie together, *religare*) with its implicit assumption that there is a human agency placed in the field of force and weighing with its own weight on the process, although unable to effect the ultimate connection, only witnessing and instrumenting it. Those who insist (today or in the past) on a "religionless" Christianity believe, in fact, that mediation is unnecessary, even false and invalid. In this view, God's authority can reach man directly. We must contest this notion: man is frail and thus a battlefield of contending forces, just as the child and the pupil are weak and ignorant unless brought into mediated (through family and school) contact with society, civilization, systematic knowledge, and competence. Like family and school, the church is an indispensable institution for the fullness of man's spiritual life in view of salvation. It is an infantile concept of freedom, writes the great theologian-philosopher Hans Urs von Balthasar, which views authority in the church as aggressive, and which imagines that one can be an "adult" vis-à-vis the church, a man in no need of advice and guidance. The Holy Spirit and His charismas mean that everybody must occupy his place and exercise the responsibilities that befall him within an organization. The responsibilities to which Christ appointed the church are not limited in time, and their exercise does not limit the freedom of the Christian.

Again we see that authority occupies a definite place in the scheme of things, and that one authority does not destroy another, it only limits it so that the organization might be adequately structured. The whole is ordered in view of the objective. It was observed before that the parent has a wide range of means at his disposal in the process of bringing the child to the realization of his social nature; the teacher's range is somewhat narrower because his field of action is only a segment of the child's social nature; the rest of the field is ordered by higher than social impulses: the attainment of knowledge for its own sake, the enlargement of the educational horizon, a historical integration with mankind's destiny through scholarly endeavors. The religious objective is the narrowest, although it embraces every act of life; through it, the individual is integrated with the economy of salvation through moral acts which, however, are not only acts between man and his fellowmen, but also and primarily between him and God. The church is the agency of God for reaching this objective; hence, it both can and cannot have the parent's almost unlimited patience with the disobeying child. It *can,* because God is infinitely merciful; it *cannot,* because offense against God is graver than against fellowmen, although very often the first is measured in terms of the second as its immediately apprehensible yardstick.

Let us bear in mind that in one way or another all religions posit an original offense by man against God which explains that (a) man is in a state of sin vis-à-vis the divine being, and (b) he needs to be coerced in his mundane transactions in order to resist his selfish, sinful impulses. Whatever we think of original sin, we are stopped and made to reflect by Pascal, who said that it is the most inexplicable thing, yet without it we can explain nothing in man's behavior. If it had not happened, according to Christian teaching, man would still need authority over him, but he would willingly obey. Authority would not be coercive. Yet anybody who has dealt with others from a position of command knows the resistance that human beings put up even against reasonable effort on behalf of their own aspirations. Another man of great religious genius, Kierkegaard, wrote that "the misfortune of our age . . . is disobedience, unwillingness to obey." He added the penetrating diagnosis:

> One deceives oneself and others by wishing to make us imagine that it is doubt. No, it is insubordination: it is not doubt of religious truth, but insubordination against religious authority which is the fault in our misfortune and the cause of it. Disobedience is the secret of the religious confusion of our age.[10]

Doubt would be situated somewhere along the line of intellectual probing; insubordination to religious authority is of a moral-spiritual nature, the very root of sin, thus, the root also from which the need for authority sprouts. But there is a further implication of the Kierkegaardian passage, going yet deeper, even though not necessarily in harmony with all religious thought. Kierkegaard suggests that insubordination arises not because the religious authority does not know how to reason against doubt. It arises because in the nineteenth (and we may add, the twentieth) century, amidst spreading religious indifference, religious authority argues, reasons, explains, thus becomes flat, tied to argumentation, and becomes finally nothing but a school of thought, increasingly mundane. Religious authority, in other words, must be exercised, and not merely give reasons

41

why it should be obeyed. It is a church, not a school, and it should not behave like one. I said a moment ago that Kierkegaard's position in this matter may not be acceptable to all religious thinkers who hold that religious faith needs also the support of reason. Yet, the Danish thinker put his finger on an essential point in regard to the true nature of authority, religious or otherwise. Mediation must always take into consideration who is at the receiving end of the process. In the case of religion the receptor is usually a recalcitrant creature, more recalcitrant than in other cases. In the latter, the "rewards" for conforming with authority are immediate and obvious; in the former, the rewards are intangible. The use of authority, we see it again, follows not only from the nature of the emitter of the message, or from the nature of the message, but also from the nature of those to whom it is addressed. In this regard, man is an authority-bound being.[11]

The awesome character of religious authority does not leave for churches another stance—and another type of institutional organization —than a highly exacting one, thus strongly stamped by authority. Again, an analogy may be drawn with family and school. Society may make room for the spoiled child and the uneducated adult, yet this laxity does not empower parents and teachers to be lax with their own tasks. As mediators, they have to convey the entire "social message" to child and pupil, and make sure that it is assimilated. Similarly the church: God's mercy is finally up to him to apportion, but the church must see that His commandments are kept, hopefully with the complete adherence of heart and mind.

As in education and in family life, there is today a serious crisis in religious life, too. It was mentioned before that religion itself is sought to be abolished; the demand is based upon the claim that religion blocks the free flow of God's charisma to man. Together with this crisis of religion (in reality, of the concept of *mediation*), there is, logically, a crisis of priesthood, of seminaries, of episcopal and papal authority. The reason may be schematized by saying that the concept of mediation, thus of authority, is under a formidable attack. Remove the "institutional" church, the doctrine, the formal prayers, and so on, the critics insist, and let God call every man. What follows in such cases of removal of mediating authority? A repetition of what happened in the universities after 1968: not an honest effort at abolishing authority (human nature excludes it), merely a shift. In the universities the shift has been from scholarship to reckless ideology, from an elite to demagogues; in religious matters the logic of abolition of the institutional church can only lead to a shift in authority from God to man. More precisely, to the religious indifference of the vast majority hardly compensated for by the personal enthusiasm of a few whose spirituality, no longer channeled, propels self-love to the ultimate excess: self-divinization. According to our constant comparison, the religionless faithful (the "Christians without a church" in Leszek Kolakowski's description) would be like the child who usurps the parent's role or the pupil who thinks he possesses knowledge.[12] The comparison is inadequate only in the sense that the paradox to which it points is necessarily too weak to convey the much more grievous paradox of the self-idolator.[13]

The nature of the religious crisis is, then, the crisis of authority, or, as Kierkegaard wrote, of insubordination. Those who ought to exercise it have succumbed to a basic fallacy and are now merely going the full length of the consequent chain reaction. The man (or the institution) who fails to use authority when entrusted with it does not believe, in the depth of his heart, that he uses it legitimately. Legitimacy, in his already changed heart, belongs to the opponents, to history, to the future. He himself is entrusted with its liquidation, so that soon afterwards a more legitimate, even though contrary, situation might arise. In the particular instance of today's religious crisis the holders of authority are convinced that the only legitimate situation is the *disuse of authority,* thus of institution, tradition, mediation. Hence, the anarchy at episcopal conferences and pastoral synods, the interdict cast on the Tridentine mass, the game of change played with the liturgy, the mocking of the sacraments. So-called "experimental groups" inherit the authority thus dispersed, but can do nothing with it since they, too, are now impregnated with the authority-holders' gnawing suspicion that there is no divine authority behind theirs. If so, then salvation is nothing but a myth and mediation a travesty. The institutional framework of the church may remain, but as a secular social agency. The best analogy would be that of a family without love or a school without respect for knowledge.

There are those who reason post facto about the present religious crisis, and who might adopt Carl Friedrich's argument: "As a tradition becomes ritualized, and hence a symbol, it may gain in emotional appeal what it lacks in specific content. As it does, it loses force as a basis for authority, since reasoning cannot be based upon a symbol."[14] I choose this passage because it represents a diametrically opposite interpretation of religion from that of Kierkegaard. The Danish theologian's general thrust was that religion involves man's existential decision, his entire commitment, in which reason itself plays a secondary role. What he meant by "subordination" to God's call and command (see his lifelong preoccupation with Abraham's readiness to sacrifice Isaac) was the bending of the whole personality without reservations, particularly without arguments, subtle *distinguos,* or debates. Professor Friedrich falls into the opposite error, although he does not address himself in the

43

quoted passage to the issue of religion: he makes authority exclusively dependent on reason, and reason, he writes, cannot be based upon a symbol. Hence, authority, when ritualized with the help of symbols, loses its content, although it may gain emotional appeal.

But authority, while directing men to objectives compatible with their rationality, is not an argumentative mechanism. It appeals to reason, but it also appeals to the will, especially in religious matters where a warped will (original sin) must be solicited even more firmly than the dissenting mind. The objective is not, of course, to break the will, but to gain its consent by various means which include judicious coercion. Actually, nothing better has been found in mankind's experience than the *training of habit,* which is also the formal character of education, manners, civilized attitudes, and even of higher virtues. In this sense, authority is a permanent reminder, thus a reinforcer, of habits; since habits, however, spring from an initial conscious acceptance followed by an internalized automatization, it may be said that authority aims at the *ritualization of good habits.*[15] Disagreeing with Carl Friedrich, we argue that ritualized and symbol-laden tradition is a strong requirement of authority, the more so as we proceed from a small, well-linked group like the family, to larger and heterogeneous groups like the community of believers in a church or the citizens of a nation. The rites and symbols make up for the unity that is lacking in the group where individuals do not know each other. And these rites and symbols are the more effective as their origin reaches further back, because then the participants feel linked to each other not only horizontally, but also to the long line of ancestors in the past and descendants in the future. Thus authority is reinforced in several dimensions; one might say that rites and symbols possess authority just as the individuals when entrusted with it.

Innovation which brutally breaks with tradition lets authority hang on the single tenuous thread of a human being's decision, and cuts the even more important thread of consecrated rites and symbols. Cardinal Newman, defining "true development" of doctrine, laid down some of the ground rules of authority also:

> ... true development may be described as one which is conservative of the course of antecedent developments, being really those antecedents and something else besides them; it is an addition which illustrates, not obscures, corroborates, not corrects, the body of thought from which it proceeds; and this is its characteristic as contrasted with a corruption.[16]

(d) Authority and the Courts

According to Max Weber's distinction, while power is essentially tied to the personality of individuals, authority is always associated with so-

44

cial positions and roles; therefore, authority is legitimate power. We may say then that such a power is derived from existing laws, including the law which determines the mode of selecting the holders of authority. Let us also note another pertinent distinction, made by the Belgian philosopher, Marcel De Corte: all groups have rules, only political society has laws. And when we speak of courts, we have the judicial authority in mind, an authority from whose scope no one born under those laws is exempt—while the rules of other groups within the same nation do not have a legitimate coercive power behind them. One may voluntarily resign from membership in a group and reject the rules; one may not live outside the laws of a nation. Laws, then, have a uniquely coercive power, and since they have it by rational design, itself embedded on the one hand in tradition, on the other in natural law, they possess the fullness of authority.

The debate seems to be endless to establish whether the law has its own legitimacy, derived from a preexisting, universally valid, natural law, or whether its sole legitimacy lies in the fact that it expresses a temporary consensus of citizens who may change it whenever and however they wish. Enough has been said so far of authority for us to grasp the essential character of the law: it is rooted in man's rational and social nature, and it belongs to the essence of a structured community. If laws are often referred to as guideposts, this indicates their function to remind people of their social limits in the absence of instincts which are the animal's limitations and guideposts. Yet, it is an error to say, as many sociologists and jurists do, that societies have now reached a point in their evolution where the anonymous "rule of law" can replace all other relationships, mainly based on authority. We would rather argue that the law is never separable from authority, and that if the citizen obeys the law, it is not so much this or that concretely formulated law he obeys, as his rational conviction that laws are for the good of the community of which he is a member, and that the community itself stands above the positive laws. How could we otherwise explain that we obey injunctions not set down in law books? How could we explain the existence, for example, of respect for elders, of considerateness in our dealings, and simply of manners? How could we explain, furthermore, that we are willing to change laws but not the nation, and are ready to sacrifice our lives for the nation, although such a sacrifice cannot ultimately be enforced by laws? Authority, written or unwritten, permeates all our social manifestations; the written law is only one segment of such manifestations, formalized and enforced, to be sure, but deriving support from a deeper source. A prominent contemporary sociologist, not known for his weddedness to tradition, asserts that "authority is a more universal element of social structure than even property and status."[17]

All this is not meant to underestimate the role of judicial authority; on the contrary, we see its roots in man's social rationality in a clearer light.

Yet, the one striking characteristic about law is that, unlike family, school, and church, which lead us to something positive and expect positive acts, the law's and the court's essential function is to *forbid,* to tell us *prima facie* what we should not do. In this, however, the law does not contradict its society-building, society-preserving, rational character: the forbidden act is a reminder of our social-rational integration by the same token as the positive acts that morality and, hence, the law, too, enjoin us to perform. The moral law is binding because we are endowed with the knowledge of good and evil, even though this knowledge must be reinforced by divine revelation and commandments, and by the action of moral authority; positive law is likewise binding because it is a parallel articulation of relationships which, although their scene is society, fall under the rubric of the moral law. It is the character of the law—its immediately grasped double origin and double relevance: in moral consciousness *and* need for social protection—which makes of the authority enforcing it something awesome. Today, we do not notice it too clearly because the work of the judicial authority, the courts, and the penal agencies are hygienically kept from the public eye; but let us remember that until recently the judicial act was not only public and publicized, it was also at the center—governmental and geographical center—of the community's life.[18] Justice was concretely and personally meted out by kings, whether Solomon or Saint Louis; executions were designed to serve as terrifying examples; the executioner himself was regarded as a half-sacred, half-monstrous agent of a power itself placed, on such occasions, on the edge of the human and the divine. Joseph de Maistre in his political dialogues sees the executioner as the axis of the State on whose high works (*hautes oeuvres*) everything else rests.

Judicial authority is then essentially protective of the social fabric, and it is articulated according to this function alone. What would be, indeed, the significance of family, school, State, army, and so on if these socially integrating and civilizing institutions were made to contemplate a bottomless opening at the other end, so to speak?[19] Why educate, civilize, and protect, when those who ignore these objectives and attempt to destroy their efficiency go unpunished? Such a dissymmetry would be entirely intolerable; as a matter of fact, judicial and legal permissiveness have as an immediate consequence not only an increase in the crime rate, but also the dissolution of other institutions. The nature of sanctions is that it is indivisible: if those who deserve it are not appropriately penalized, then the so-far guiltless tend to fall, by a kind of social gravitational pull, to lower levels of discipline and civilization. This tendency renders the debate about the merits of punishment in general, and of capital punishment in particular, idle. The courts do not punish merely to deter would-be criminals from committing a crime; they do so for two other reasons also:

46

the first is that the breaking of the law is an offense against the moral-social equilibrium which must be restored; the second, following from the preceding one, is that unpunished criminal acts weaken institutional authority all along the line. Do we need a better reminder that society is a network of imitation almost too subtle to detect, and in which only the cooperation of all institutions is able to maintain social rationality, that is, the rational need to live in community?

The breakdown of judicial authority is today notorious. Crime in the streets and skyjacking are only two varieties of myriad acts of terror against which governments, courts, municipalities and police seem powerless. As always when confronted with such phenomena, we must ask what do the men entrusted with judicial authority think of their function? The answer is not hard to find. The prevailing view is that (Western) society is undergoing a mutation from one structure to another, from authoritarian to egalitarian, from institutional to fraternal, from firm to loose. Modern judges tend to shy away from sentencing according to laws which seem now rigid, static. They sentence in the spirit of "new laws," not yet codified but already adopted by the "new society" as its program and life-style. There are judges in America who openly declare that all justice is "class justice" and that they (a Midwestern judge comes to mind) intend to acquit young members of the counterculture when charged; there are judges in France who routinely decide in favor of defendants of lower classes and personally arrest employers with handcuffs where a worker is injured as a result of a factory accident. The "bad conscience" or "guilt complex" that Western society and its judicial agencies allegedly suffer from is not so much a matter of conscience and feeling of guilt as the sense of a historical shift toward another historical form, the dim awareness of a civilizational change (called mutation or evolution) from Judeo-Christian morality and its classical conceptualization toward an emerging set of ideas and beliefs, not yet formulated. Take as a pertinent illustration the views of Jean-Paul Sartre on crime, as expressed in *Saint Genet, Comedian and Martyr,* one of his most revealing works. Sartre argues that there is no such thing as a thief or a murderer because the individual performing the act does not have the consciousness of committing evil. Only bourgeois morality, always on the lookout for scapegoats, labels these acts "theft" and "murder," thereby providing a convenient victim for the protection of its own bourgeois interests. Philosophically, this means that objective reality does not exist, only what is reflected in the subjective mind; from the point of view of justice and law enforcement, we find in Sartre's analysis one of the roots of the criminals' and lawyers' so frequent plea that responsibility for the incriminating act should be attributed to society, to institutional violence, to political motives. Objective guilt and the consciousness of being guilty (as contrasted

47

with a vague *feeling* of guilt) are now notions made to vanish by a sleight of hand in which judicial authority cooperates, increasingly convinced that the truth of these notions has been dissolved by the new modes of thought, psychoanalysis, existentialism, Marxism.

Almost the whole question rests, consequently, on the underlying belief that a new society can be constructed in which no tribunals will be necessary because subjective conviction (if "sincerely" held) is always guiltless. This separation of guilt from the individual permits guilt to be ascribed haphazardly to any social or political entity, and at any rate to be dissolved among the many subjectivities, including the judge's own, who is accused of following his class or race prejudices when passing sentence. Needless to say, it also renders the courts superfluous, as we see from such signs as the increasing importance of psychologists and psychiatrists at investigations and trials. The logic of the situation would lead, if unchecked, to the replacement of courts by committees consisting of psychological and sociological experts presided over by the criminal himself who, after all, knows best his own case! It leads, in other words, to the elimination of the judge's mediating function, and conceptually, to the denial of a higher law which must be mediated and articulated to the members of the community. The parallel with the other institutions, already discussed, is obvious; in every case the crisis can be shown to spring from the attempt to eliminate the *mediating agent* and reduce the "space" between the source of authority and those supposed to obey it, to zero. Father, teacher, priest, and judge see their roles indefinitely weakened; the trend is in each case for an elected committee to take their place, itself to be replaced *in fine* by the individual's consciousness.[20] The child, the pupil, the believer, the criminal are credited with possessing the best insight into their own motives (as if this were the decisive point) and *therefore* the only correct judgment on the merits of their acts. In reality, the systematic critique to which the mediating agent is today subjected, and behind him the entire concept of mediation, indicates that the critics reject the notion that there is anything to be mediated: natural law, divine will, or a body of knowledge. The irony of the resulting situation is that the anti-mediation process is never allowed to run its full course; it is arrested before individual conscience would actually take over. Who interferes?

The enemies of authority are particularly vehement in their savage attack on the court, the most exposed social defense line against subversion. Note that in every Western country large majorities demand severe sentences against the new types of aggressors, terrorists, urban guerrillas, kidnappers, and so on. It makes no difference that this demand is made along democratic popular channels, popular votes or referenda: it is rejected with indignation by a vocal minority in parliaments, by the media, by the always-ready defenders of permissiveness. A few years ago in Great Britain, a country not known for hotheaded and extremist mores, a large majority of the population expressed itself for capital punishment in certain serious cases such as the killing of unarmed policemen. Parliament rejected it without argument, merely because some prominent Labor members felt that this would be barbarous in the twentieth century. Practically identical opinions were expressed in the fall of 1975 over the execution of five terrorists in Spain who had killed policemen. I quote from a Berlin newspaper, the *Tagesspiegel* (September 27) as a typical reaction:

> Some of the condemned come from anarchist movements which condone terror themselves, and the accusation of the murder of a policeman weighs heavily. But there are such movements in many countries without the State being forced on this account to become an executioner . . . . In civilized States today, the right to revenge the shedding of blood by shedding blood is not allowed.

It is doubtful whether the writer of these lines has reflected sufficiently on what constitutes civilization. It is more probable that he subscribes unthinkingly to a historically observable phenomenon, namely that a certain category of people stands above the law; it is *privileged.* Temporarily, the privileged are young people, from rioting students to urban guerrillas, but their exceptional status is not defined in law as it was in past historical epochs, nor is it subject to a severe law among peers; it is a savage state of affairs justified by the intellectual terror of otherwise well-behaved ideologues behind their desks. Tomorrow another class of people may be so favored by the same or other ideologues, enemies of authority and subverters of institutions. The situation leads to the one described by Solzhenitsyn in the *Gulag Archipelago*, the concept of a State based entirely on "class justice," the tribunals acting exclusively in the interest of the Soviet regime, supreme expression of the dictatorship of the proletariat.

(e) Authority in the Workshop

During the roughly two centuries of liberalism, authority in the workshop and factory was not a problem; it did not figure either in works on economics nor in political discussions. The Biblical injunction that Adam had to earn his bread by the "sweat of his brow" was also assumed to mean that workers are, by their condition and social status, not owners of the enterprise in which they work. True, the medieval English poem asked the pointed question: "When Adam delved and Eve span, who was then the gentleman?" This merely suggested that it is immoral to live idly while others exert themselves. This is compatible with the demand for higher wages and better working conditions, but it does not imply "ownership of the means of production" by the workers themselves. It is also compatible with the enterprise being run in view of production, run in a hierarchical manner, and with decisions about productivity, layoff of personnel, reinvestment of profit, and so on, made by the owner alone. Marx himself admitted that social or communal labor on a large scale requires leadership; both he and Engels mocked the anarchists and asked how can a locomotive, for example, be run collectively.

At least one outstanding modern economist, Joseph Schumpeter, called attention to the military character of big industry and argued that the industrial revolution would not have been so successful if the workers, recently still peasants and brought up in a reverential (feudal) mentality, had not regarded the entrepreneur the way their ancestors had regarded the lord or his intendant for centuries, indeed millenaries. At the same time, Schumpeter saw this mentality on the wane, under the pressure of the steady democratization and leveling of political life—a pressure created by the entrepreneurial class, too—which gradually emancipated the workers also. If not yet political voters with full rights, the workers "voted" as consumers. Soon the full weight of their political and union pressure was added to their consumership. At any rate, the multiplying reform movements swept the agricultural world—land reform, distribution of land, dividing up of large estates and plantations—and powerfully affected the bastions of industrial life; the latest demand is the association of workers to management, indeed, to ownership, of factories. The English socialist John Strachey provided perhaps the most radical formulation, short of Marx's own, of the rationale behind the various forms of *cogestion* and *autogestion* (France) and *Mitbestimmung* (Germany): since political power follows from economic power, Strachey argued, the complete equalization of property owning would result in political equalization, a situation where no man possessed power over another man.

Strachey was a Fabianist and a Labor Party intellectual. However, his point of view, with variations, is that of the socialists generally. More recently, Professor Richard Lowenthal voiced a terminologically more up-to-date theory, the implication of which is that socialism has conquered the Western industrial mind and has become the semiofficial point of view of advanced industrial society. Lowenthal's argument is that such a society is so powerful that the danger is it might fall into the hands of the

50

politically strong State. The only guarantee that this will not happen is the participation of the citizens at all levels of power and decision-making. The more complete democracy we have, the lower the probability that power becomes concentrated in a few hands, particularly in the hands of the politically mighty. Lowenthal's logic, like Strachey's, ought to lead him to the equal distribution of property, particularly in the case of vast industrial enterprises lest they establish a strong partnership with State power since the temptation is strong on both sides.

We may now ask the question about the nature of authority in the workshop. Without agreeing either with John Strachey or with Richard Lowenthal, it is a good application of the principle of subsidiarity to hold that all men ought to own property. Not because this would lead to the abolition of "one man's power over another": such a thing is neither possible, nor desirable, and it certainly would not come about as a result of universal property ownership. Property ownership is a good thing because a man's freedom includes his economic freedom. It extends, so to speak, his sphere of self-protection and action, the intangible circle inside which he feels secure against sickness, mishaps, and financial and political pressure. But this does not mean that if everybody owned the same amount or value of property, there would be no envy and desire to own better things, to own what the neighbor has. So even if all men owned property, some property would be larger, better situated, better managed, more profitable, and so forth, than others; inequality would not cease, in this domain or in others, and the nature of society would remain such that inevitably more power would be held by A than by B.[21] Thus, the rational nature of society, which, we repeat, implies the acceptance of inequality as both natural and a means of preventing a totalitarian steam-roller reducing everybody to serfdom, contradicts the premise that all men ought to own the same amount of property. In the specific case of industrial enterprises, this principle holds as good as in every other case. First, because part-ownership of the enterprise by all personnel would decrease its efficiency, which is the implicit objective of the enterprise, and which would be all the more essential as the part-owners' stake in it would be now greater. I assume, namely, that under conditions of co-ownership the individual worker or employee would invest (reinvest) part of his earnings voluntarily or by common decision, so that his sustenance would now depend to a greater degree on the enterprise's profitable operations. This happy result would, however, be doubtful under collective management.

But management would not be collective, declare the partisans of co-ownership; an elected group of workers would fully participate in decision-making, together with the original owners. Experience shows in ev-

51

ery country where this method was tried that the workers' representatives soon began identifying themselves with the owners and handling the rank-and-file workers' interest no better than these owners, perhaps even a bit more harshly. Besides, who are these worker-representatives? They are union members in good standing, and their newly acquired associate-entrepreneurial power merely increases the power of the unions within the enterprise. Thus, our second point is that the result of co-ownership leaves the workers with less power than before when they benefited from the "dual regime" in which both entrepreneur and union competed for their allegiance. In the name of an illusory economic co-determination, they would have a united and accrued power-complex over their heads.[22]

To hold economic power over one's fellow men is neither, by itself, exploitative as Marx holds, nor an obstacle for the less powerful (less rich, less competent, in lower rank) to engage in economic pursuits elsewhere or at other times. Nothing prevents an American worker occupying a certain job in an enterprise from investing his earnings and acquiring income and status higher than that which corresponds to his base position. In Europe, foreign workers (Turks, Italians, Yugoslavs, Spaniards, Portuguese, Algerians) occupied in industries in Germany, France, Belgium, or Switzerland end up with an increased status at home where they return after years of work in more developed countries. There is no reason why some of these men, putting their savings together, should not invest this aggregate capital in a new venture in which they are owners, managers, and personnel.

Our consideration of authority in the workshop aims then exclusively at enterprises where the traditional structure prevails and where ownership, management, and work force constitute economically and managerially distinct entities. The purpose of authority in an industrial enterprise is *efficiency*—and not necessarily profit, since there are cases when the products are not sold but distributed or destined for self-sufficiency, self-defense, charity, and so on.[23] "Efficiency" itself is another term for quality, inventiveness, the right time requisite for manufacturing or producing the object, the coordination of efforts, competence, grasp of purpose, and what may be called satisfaction in one's work. All these components of the process of producing goods of whatever nature—and there may be others such as satisfying of the workers' various needs called today "fringe benefits"—make of the industrial enterprise a social, not merely an economic, unit. *Social* here means a complex undertaking which serves, to be sure, the purpose of its own satisfaction, but also purposes outside itself. Just like the family, which is self-contained, yet it prepares children for a wider social vocation. The enterprise could not fulfill *its* vocation if it, too, were not structured according to the broadly understood principle of efficiency. The latter is the "higher law" of the enterprise, a law which proposes the legitimate satisfaction of people's needs for merchandise; it is these needs which must order and articulate its internal arrangements, its hierarchy, the setting of proximate or distant objectives. Authority may be lodged in one man or in a small group, but it cannot be shared by all or equally.

These observations would be obvious if the idea of the industrial society, for the past two centuries a ubiquitous reality, had not warped our sense of proportions. As Karl Polanyi has written, Western man and in his wake the rest of mankind, including the Marxists, were led to assume that industrial production, efficiency, and consumerism are the ultimate aims of society. The sudden and spectacular prosperity that befell a good part of mankind in the nineteenth century has veiled from our eyes the fact that society is now ruled by an ideology, the industrial ideology, which has persuaded us that societies and nations ought also to be organized on the principle of efficiency without which there would be no industry in the modern sense. *Man* became equated with *worker,* and governments are chiefly preoccupied with matters that pertain to the business of business executives. One hears almost nothing else from the mouth of politicians than "gross national product," full employment, deficit spending, monetary reform, balance of payments—which is quite natural in a State conceived as an enterprise, but becomes a symptom of a grievous disequilibrium if one hears nothing about moral issues, the embellishment of cities, concern with religion, the aesthetic and the corporate components of life.

Under these circumstances, authority in the enterprise is either diluted among the many eager aspirants, or it abandons its social function and retreats into a self-centered, self-contained position. The first case may, of course, explain the second: the entrepreneur is hardly allowed to run his enterprise, which is hemmed in by the never ending demands of unions, fiscal authorities, pressure groups, various crusades, and the media. By definition, the enterprise is in the focus of industrial society; it is easy to blame it for practically all social mishaps and failures, since its stamp on people's lives is indeed the deepest.[24] Who can be said to possess authority in this case? How can the entrepreneur take it upon himself to articulate the goals of his enterprise when at every step his intentions and plans are interfered with—and not in the name of the common good, but in the name of pressure groups whose combined action would still not amount to socially constructive ends?

On the other hand, the entrepreneur's temptation is great to make of his enterprise an autonomous unit, even if the pressures on him were tolerable. The days of America's civic-minded businessmen seem to be over. We witness instead the withdrawal of big corporations into the "wilderness," away from cities and even beyond the suburbs, where the company may mushroom on its own like a feudal fief with laws and a way of life, and search for the ultimate self-contained efficiency. Such companies, the giants among them, cover the country with a network reminiscent of a separate sovereign nation. High echelon officials (and of course their families) are subject to frequent mobilization from one power center to another, with such effects as loss of roots, habits, and community acceptance. The term ":company wife" shows exactly the devastating nature of the phenomenon.

Squeezed between the two gigantic pressures, outside interference and its own bigness, the enterprise in the industrial society is no longer an institution where one could use the word "authority" with any clear meaning. This unfortunate evolution does not alter the fact, however, that *work* is ordered to a social achievement and that it is conditioned by an organization which exists in view of the work-entity's proximate end. The restoration of authority in the enterprise depends, probably, on a return to manageable size, away from the forces which covet it as a power base. This would suggest that the "socialization of the means of production" is a wrong solution; but perhaps more than the present status quo is needed for the right solution: a retreat from the industrial society.

(f) Authority in Literature and Art

In the last two centuries the Western world has come to believe that artists, writers, and intellectuals are a separate breed, somehow not quite belonging to society, but floating on its margins and slightly above. This belief is in notorious contrast with that of all other places and times, and it does not necessarily speak for the correctness of the modern attitude. Ancient Greek and medieval artists, in fact, artists up until the eighteenth century, were regarded as artisans, more talented than others of their confreres, but artisans nevertheless. The writers, unless they possessed independent means, were mainly in the employ of the noble, the rich, the monasteries, and the guilds. The same was true of "intellectuals," called at the time clerks; none of them had even the shadow of political power, and their influence on the small reading, cultured public was derived strictly from their ability to entertain, to plumb the depth of the human soul and to use in the service of these goals a clear language and a beautiful style.

It is by no means a coincidence that a different situation developed with the rise of the industrial-commercial middle class, of democracy, and mass civilization. As economic activities and speculation about them became the center of interest, the artistic and literary competence and concern of the earlier higher classes, resulting in active sponsorship, yielded to the distracted and incompetent attitude of the bourgeoisie. The artist and the writer found themselves suddenly without a public, because what the new public now wanted were popular newspapers, melodramas, exciting stories, and the rest of a budding mass culture. Thus, artists and writers were pushed aside, even though at the same time a sense of embarrassment also placed them on a pedestal. The pedestal proved to be a platform of irresponsibility since the artists now felt that they were only marginal to society's central concerns. The dissociation of art and society was consummated by the end of the last century with theories justifying the "ivory tower," "art for art's sake," "abstract painting," and so on.

Consequently, the delicate problem has arisen, and has grown urgent in our time, whether society is in any way justified to exercise control over art, literature, and intellectual activity. The question is asked about a wide range of issues, from the professor's academic freedom, through the journalist's right to scrutinize the lives of public figures, to the freedom of publishers and filmmakers to display pornography in books and movies. We should understand that in earlier societies such a question would have been meaningless since the artist, the clerk, and the litterateur, integrated with the rest of their fellow citizens in the mesh of the social fabric, bore the same responsibility and were subject to the same mores as any other person. Disagreement often raged about the limits of the permissible, but a common universe of discourse and the so-called shared values did indicate to all, and with a sufficient clarity when they crossed these limits, the norms of good taste, of religious faith, or moral decency.

Often, although by no means always, these limits were institutionalized as *censorship*. Let us be clear about the fact that this was not necessarily a localizable office with functionaries reading everything published or with supervisory committees visiting the artist's workshop to examine whether his latest products met the prevailing standards. The artist and writer were integrated with the world of faith and ideas around them, and although like other men they, too, had nonconforming ideas, they did not necessarily regard it as a "violation of their rights" if such ideas did not get publicized. It was this awareness of human and social limits which permeated their consciousness, the realization that the individual member of society is not the absolutely free arbiter of the permissible and the forbidden. Even as late as the seventeenth century, "people were unanimous in seeing men only as groups," writes historian Pierre Goubert.

> Man in isolation appears to them both inconceivable and disgraceful, and they barely stop short of suspecting him of sinister plans such as traffic with the Devil. In fact, even those who might today be called fringe or asocial elements—broadly speaking, the beggars of the time—seldom function as individual units and make up highly organized groups with their own leaders, laws, areas, and language.[25]

Traditionally, society divided itself into corporations the task of which was to provide members with professional or trade associations, to be sure, but also with other guideposts on the highway of life.

There were numerous famous cases of rebellion against some form or other of censorship. Let us only cite those of Socrates, accused of impiety, of Galileo, compelled to rename his theories mere hypotheses, of Baudelaire (1857), reproached for the immorality of his volume of poems *The Flowers of Evil,* and so on.[26] In the course of history there have been, naturally, many more cases of resistance to censorship, even if we confine our illustration to the relatively free Western world and leave aside the various "Oriental" and other despotisms. It is thus clear that given, on the one hand, the artist's normal and mutually beneficial social integration, and, on the other hand, his repeated rebellions against being censored, there is room within which we may investigate the problem of authority in its relation to art, literature, and the intellectual endeavor, generally.

We take it for granted in these pages that the artist is a member of society like anybody else for the simple reason that art, literature, and intellectual activity belong to the lives of all men and to the life of a well-ordered society. We reject, in other words, the utilitarian view that art, literature, culture are a kind of added decor, luxury items after other needs are satisfied; and we also reject the Marxist view that art must be subjected to total State control since it can serve, must serve, as a stimulus for productivity. There remains, however, the fact that artists do not generally constitute a group, or when they do, it is an informal movement brought together by a similarity of style, inspiration, or insight. It is never a network like the school or the workshop; it is never structured like the family. Can one speak, under these conditions, of a common purpose and of a structural inequality that a specific type of authority would have to implement?

The answer, if we put the question this way, is obviously negative. In the performance of their work, the artists, the writers, and the scholars are not subject to social authority; authority, in their case, is first exercised by the discipline inherent in their creative-productive process, a discipline following from the nature of the tools used (stone, sound, form, language, ideas), and by the line of predecessors who influence them, giving an added meaning to their own actions. *In this sense,* the artists, and so forth, cannot be said to be marginal to society; yet they are distinct from it and from its institutions. While the school can teach, theoretically, any bona fide student, while the workshop produces freely exchangeable goods, while all citizens are responsible to the laws represented by the courts, the artist's work is unique, not exchangeable, not imitable, and, strictly speaking, it cannot be cited before an "artist's tribunal," there to be found innocent or guilty.

Yet, there is *another sense* also in which the artist's work and the social response intersect, more than that, they overlap. That is where we must look for the function of authority. The chief task of the workshop is to combine the participants in an efficient production; it is this priority which legitimates authority in the industrial enterprise. Is there a chief task of art, literature, and scholarship? It is the pursuit of truth and beauty, first for the sake of truth and beauty themselves, secondly for their insertion into social existence. We must be careful with our perhaps too subtle distinction: we do not conceive of society as an inert aggregate in which individuals alone are alive; society as a moral person is alive as such; it, too, pursues truth and beauty; it is not merely their beneficiary through the presence in its midst of artists and writers. We thus distinguish two aspects of the artists' task, but merely to suggest that truth and beauty order society's aesthetic component in like manner that law, for example, orders its intrinsic sense of justice (intrinsic because there can be no society with freedom to commit acts against it). We said earlier that authority mediates between a higher law and the individual by articulating the higher law in terms of expected behavior, if possible, internalized, turned into a self-improving conviction. Truth and beauty represent the higher law for artists and scholars inasmuch as their best efforts ought to reflect man to himself, not like a mirror image, rather like a portrait: in his unsuspected fullness. If this is attained, then the artist can be said to insert truth and beauty in the life of society at whatever scale and dimension he does his work; if he pursues other ends, he fails to fulfill his social responsibility and the question may be discussed whether and in what ways authority should be applicable to him.

Viewed from the angle of society, the artist is society's guide to certain values, in the same way as the worker and entrepreneur are guides to obtain certain goods.[27] We would not usually make our garments or automobiles; we turn to tailors and car manufacturers for these objects. We turn to the architect, the composer, the poet, and the scholar to obtain their creations. Truth and beauty are the foundations of our confidence in artists, just as efficiency is the foundation of our trust in the tailor and the car manufacturer. Why should the artist not be brought within the scope of his responsibility, not in the same but in an analogous manner to the tailor's and car maker's responsibility?

This might be said to be a pedestrian, indeed, a utilitarian approach to higher, nonmeasurable things in which the individual should not be called into account. For example, André Gide, accused of being a bad influence on his readers when he endorsed homosexuality, replied that once the writer launches his work, he cares not at all what its fate may be. This is obviously a wrong answer, and it casts a different light on the approach I am suggesting. I insisted that the higher law which authority mediates to the artist is the pursuit of beauty and truth; they are needed by society, not only by the artist and by a small elite more directly appreciating his work. So we ought, if we can, to judge the artist's work precisely within his own universe of discourse and because it is vitally important for our aesthetic well-being. In other words, censorship cannot be regarded either as a no longer relevant institution belonging to past unenlightened ages, or as a scandalous encroachment on the artist's rights.

The work of artists has always been and always will be censored. We spoke before of art sponsors who commissioned artists, discussed their plans and work, criticized or lauded them, influenced, controlled, and financed them. These art sponsors were not only individuals, but also convents, municipalities, corporations of burghers, governments, popes, guilds, and noble or wealthy families. Was this patronage good or bad? On balance, the art of the ages testifies that it was good and positive because the work of art benefited by the artist's genius as he was advised, recognized, admired, criticized, and interfered with. Or we see artists grouped in academies and judging younger ones, setting standards, making the world of recognition difficult of access so that only the best succeed. One finds the young Leonardo for a long time apprentice in Verrocchio's atelier, doing lowly jobs, working as told.

All these are forms of authority, only once removed from censorship. When such a censorship is absent, first the artist, then society pay the price of insufficient discipline, lack of preparation, unsure talent. Janick and Toulmin describe in their book *Wittgenstein's Vienna* the artistic life of the Austrian capital at the turn of the century when architecture, music, various branches of learning, and so on, were sponsored by aristocratic and wealthy bourgeois families who paid artists and scholars in their retinue as tutors for their children, orchestras for their entertainment, as architects to build their homes, summer residences, and parks. After 1920 and with the explosion of the empire, these high ranks and fortunes vanished. The artists were suddenly on their own; they began forming cliques, movements, schools, and became independent. Yet, as the authors remark, "the self-imposed constraints, in conformance with the conventions of an artistic or intellectual profession, can be just as inhibiting and damaging to the individual fantasy as external constraints, such as those imposed by the older patronage system." (p. 255.)

We are not so sure that constraints, self-imposed or external, are damaging, except in extreme cases. At any rate, the patronage system can be called a form of censorship; the distance between the two is not unbridgeable. Besides, in the debate about censorship, which is really one about authority, the issue is seldom art, literature, and scholarship. Concretely, the issue is whether the scholar as a professor may stretch academic freedom to include incitement to violence—whether the artist may exhibit copulating figures—whether the filmmaker should dwell on nakedness—

whether the architect has the right to disfigure a street or a neighborhood with disharmonious edifices? Admittedly, these cases are hard to decide upon, but my contention is that while there may be disagreement on the degree and modality of application, we must agree on the existence of limits not to be transgressed. We may argue, for example, that pornographic literature should be sold "under the counter," but not that the opening of "porno shops" should be legalized; we may hold, indeed, that the public "has a right to know," yet we may deny that it has the right to know everything.

The absence of authority in artistic and other matters leads not to a generalized, happy freedom but to the takeover of the decision-making power by those incompetent to exercise it. I use the word "incompetent" carefully: we must assume that the journalist, the artist, and the professor are competent in their respective fields, in the sense of having expertise in a technique and in the field of pertinent knowledge. They may be incompetent, however, to see vaster connections, the network of which adds up as the common good. The quality of an artist or of a scholar is no guarantee in itself for an understanding of the social-moral fabric within which he lives: the latter understanding is of a political nature. Nor is the intensity of his convictions or of his crusading spirit a sufficient reason to say that he represents a higher morality than that of his environment, or a new morality overshadowing the traditional one. When Professor Noam Chomsky, a linguist, builds for himself a pedestal out of books on foreign policy, it may be questioned whether he is right in transferring his reputation in one area to an altogether different one.

Such an exalted view about the artist's and scholar's place vis-à-vis the community is recent; it tells about the loss of integration between society and a certain category of its citizens. Those who speak so abundantly about the "alienation" of workers ought to reflect also on the alienation of artists who no longer find their social role except mostly in "revolt." But one cannot have one's cake and eat it: if we are for the dis-alienation of the artist, we are for his integration. And that means some form of control over his art, in other words, censorship.

(g) Authority in the Army

The choice of these section heads sufficiently indicates that this book moves within the framework of those institutions which, even though they may greatly vary in form from one epoch and civilization to another, are fundamental to life in community and therefore, to rational life. The historian Georges Dumézil, whose area of study is Indo-European society, its structure, and its myths, concluded some years ago that Indo-

Europeans function on a tripartite pattern and divide their society into three classes: priests, warriors, and peasants. The same division has Plato's favor: philosopher-guides, warriors, and the working people, artisans and agriculturists. The medieval, Church-inspired social structure was also composed of those who contributed to the existence of the commonwealth by praying to God for his favor, shedding their blood in the community's defense, and working for its prosperity. In other than Indo-European societies the same phenomenon is observed, in looser forms or more rigid like the castes.

We find the defense force always present, indeed as the core of the community. The army is always at the origin of the nation itself, either through the mythical hero, or through conquest, or through the leadership of revolution and independence. The United States, too, was born in the war of independence and its first president was a general. Thus, the defense force has a high prestige; it claims some years of everybody's life, and it is a social melting pot in spite of its hierarchical character. The priority it has always enjoyed is also due to the fact that its vocation makes it transcend life itself since every soldier may lose his when in action. Our attachment to life makes us surround death and all its agents and victims with awe: the executioner is a sacred figure, yet monstrous, too, since he embodies an existential, although not legal, ambiguity: he kills a man who cannot defend himself, yet he does so as society's defense mechanism.[28] The soldier does not suffer from this ambiguity (or moral opprobrium), because he kills men who have an equal chance of killing him. Nevertheless, the preparation of a soldier, ultimately aimed at shedding blood, requires a very high degree of solidarity (esprit de corps) among the members of the army, because while society vitally needs soldiers, it also recognizes their separateness. The solidarity of which we speak is not only horizontal as among comrades-in-arm, it is vertically formalized as discipline, itself guaranteed by hierarchy. In fact, the army displays the prototype of hierarchy and discipline, for the obvious reason that in decisive moments, the moments of "life and death," the soldiers would run away without the tight moral-social injunctions that discipline and hierarchy had articulated for them at training time, in the barracks, and during instruction. The soldier does not desert because some of the strongest moral-social imperatives stand in his way: code of honor, solidarity, obedience, sacrifice. If we note them carefully, we find these injunctions operating also in society's everyday situations, but in the army they are immeasurably heightened because there they directly and visibly serve the army's collective existence and raison d'être. The civilian with a doubtful sense of honor can still function in society at large; a nonhonorable soldier is a constant threat (in the U.S. Army he is "dishonorably discharged") and his presence with all the doubt cast on him foreshadows (intolerably) his treacherous, cowardly, or simply unreliable behavior in moments of stress. He is a weak link in the chain, and the chain is not stronger than its weakest link.

Authority in the army is, consequently, the only and always thin guarantee that the whole will fulfill its mission because the parts are completely integrated. It is a thin guarantee because all the military preparation may break down in the moment of "life or death," in face of the survival instinct. Discipline (self-discipline) in important moments of life, let us say an examination or a dangerous situation, may be a sufficient requirement for a unique instant; discipline in view of death *foreseen*—and this is the essence, the "higher law," of military discipline—cannot rely on the survival instinct focused in a unique instant, it must be an acquired habit. Thus, we may define military hierarchy as the visible sign of acquired habits in the face of death. Hence the roughness of military training, its strenuous exercises and forced marches, its commands nearing at times the absurd and the useless: they aim at the intensification of the collective being, at the conviction that the whole nation is concentrated in the army, even in its smallest unit. Authority in the army is then the imposition *and* acceptance of sacrifice, the imposition and acceptance of the belief that individual soldier X is an elected part of the nation, a sacrifice offered to national survival, encompassing yet also privileging him. In the ancient world, and still in several African tribes, the king must die so as to carry his people's supreme sacrifice to the deity. Armies have always regarded themselves as performing a similar ritual.

After World War II, in the course of American-inspired democratization of German public life, the army of that nation adopted the theory of "self-leadership" (*innere Führung*); each soldier and officer was to obey only what he regarded as legitimate orders. The soldier's own conscience was to be judge of how far discipline could go—in reaction to the earlier "blind obedience" which had led, according to critics, to the carrying out of atrocious orders in Hitler's army. The consequence of "self-leadership," that is, in our terms, "self-discipline," was the collapse of discipline, the plummeting prestige of a military career, a very high percentage of conscientious objectors, and leftist agitation, including union recruitment in the barracks. The situation began to change only after 1970 when events showed that the critics of "blind" obedience, themselves in many cases university professors, obeyed orders issued not by the formidable war machine of Hitler's army, but simply by rioting student mobs who insulted and molested them, forced them out of office or made them comply with their degrading demands. If prestigious intellectuals—professors, deans, reporters—could do no better than give in to the first vulgar mob, then it must have been far more difficult to disobey harsh orders emanating from the structured chain of army command. Nevertheless, several armies have been experimenting with various degrees of "democratization": loose discipline, curbing of officers' authority, institutionalized debates of political issues in military schools and barracks, abolition of military salute, the unionization of the army, and so on.

Such "experiments" have been incorporated into military life in the United States, Holland, France, Japan, and elsewhere. Admiral Elmo Zumwalt of the U.S. Navy introduced a whole new concept of loose discipline, which then spread to the army, and to West Point. The honor code was weakened when it was suddenly found that ostracism, resulting from dishonorable conduct (for example, cheating at examinations), was "old-fashioned." As a consequence, the esprit de corps received a decisive blow, as if the innovators' purpose had been to weaken the individual link in the chain of solidarity. Life in the barracks has been made more comfortable: late hours, fewer duties, less attention paid to superiors. The latter, of all ranks, are now graded by military bureaucracy according to the amount of "trouble" in their units: racial fights, severe lack of discipline, and so forth. Like professors a decade ago, like police officials for a number of years now, army officers, too, tend now to send in false reports which show "no troubles" so as to obtain a sufficient number of "good points" for advancement and retirement. At all levels, as could be expected, the shirking of responsibility has become the tacit byword; or, to put it differently, a centrifugal attitude prevails over the concentrated one.

It is of course argued that the individual soldier feels now more like a dignified human being, no longer a cog in the machine; hence, that he performs his tasks better because he understands their scope, is free to discuss it, feels a personal responsibility for it. This is blatant untruth. We discussed before the rational aspect of authority which follows in the case on hand—from the rationality of defending one's country, from the consequent inequality of functions while this task is carried out, and from the need of discipline since man does not have the instinct of bees, which do not "desert" the hive under attack. But we also said that authority has another aspect too, not irrational, only reaching psychologically deeper. Like the child in the family, the student in school, the believer in church, the worker in the workshop, the young artist in his master's atelier—the soldier *wants* to be subordinated to discipline. This is rational, once he understands that the pertinent discipline leads to the accomplishment of the objective which defines the given institution—whereas lack of discipline dilutes the purpose and spawns incompetence. We all know, even if it is unfashionable to admit it, that the child prefers to be told what to do in school rather than follow his fancy; that the believer does not want to invent his own forms of worship; that the talented artist is aware that the pursuit of his mere inspiration, without the painfully acquired technique, leads to worthless amateurism. We also know that the soldier is not searching, as it is charged, for a so-called "father figure" when he accepts to be led according to the severest commands and is made to obey without contradiction. To what part of the soul does authority—imposed and received—respond?[29] The answer to this question was already given before, but it bears repeating in the present context. Aware that we are individuals—selfish, self-willed, "separatist"—we also long for integration in the group, including the groups which have a higher moral justification—and integrative power—than the daily gatherings at which we participate.[30] This is no nostalgia for animality, no "herd instinct" (or if it is, then it is infinitely refined and seen as a *moral* good), no mere "territorial imperative." The army, a concentrated expression of the nation, is such a group, its member feels close and loyal to what the nation is about. The orders he gives and receives are reminders and signs of the integrative process; the discipline itself creates a climate of alertness; it is a symbol of belonging to the nation, the very essence of service and sacrifice. Thus, ultimately, authority calls forth one of the deepest aspirations of man: purposeful sacrifice, which for the military, since sacrifice here is that of life itself, is daily repeated acts of discipline and authority. Let us note at this point that the more awesome the sacrifice demanded (and self-demanded) of man, the more society tends to routinize it. Liturgically precise ceremonies and rituals surround only those occasions when we come into contact with what transcends us: God, Country, Death, War, initiation into manhood, and so on. Awe (the Latin *tremendum*) is so exceptional, so overpowering that the individual is not to approach it informally and alone. The ritual is collective and meticulous, an unmistakable indication that the community feels it meets the limits of existence.

Authority in the army is, then, made up like all authority, of a rational part and another, symbol-creating part, both essential for the individual's integration with the group. Discipline, sacrifice, and solidarity are not mere external attitudes, they demand a corresponding loyalty to certain ideas. An army, for example, cannot be pacifist; while it should value peace, it cannot adopt the ideology of "peace at any price" without ceasing to be an army. Judicial authority cannot deny the necessity of punishment,[31] nor the school, that of learning, the Church, that of man's road to God. Yet we are witnessing another symptom of the breakdown of military authority in the increasingly unresisted introduction of pacifist propaganda in military academies and barracks. In the armies of Holland, France, and Italy communist publications are legally tolerated, and soldiers participating in leftist riots are not penalized. This propaganda is not merely Marxist, it aims at destroying the cohesion of the army at which it is directed. The central theme is that "capitalism is for war, socialism is for peace"; it calls attention to abuses in the barracks and in life outside, suggesting that these abuses follow from the structural evil of bourgeois society. As mentioned before, in several Western countries, including the United States, there is ever more talk of the unionization of the armed forces. This notion is as destructive of the army as pacifist ideology. As Senator John Tower says, "Imagine an army in which enlisted soldiers refuse to carry out orders from superior officers until they have been cleared by a shop steward or agreed to at a union meeting."[32]

Since the fall of 1973 antiwar activists have been lecturing at the U.S. Air Force Academy (Colorado). First arrested for distributing antiwar leaflets on campus, these activists, led by Father William Sulzman, were invited by the officials of the Academy to lecture to an ethics class. The press reports the words of Captain Richard Boyle, information officer: "It is a little emotional at first, but once the lecturer and the students decide the other side has a point, it settles down and becomes a scholarly discussion." Such discussions, scholarly or not, have no place in military academies—just as "the advantages of being uneducated" would be no suitable course for a school, and handbooks about "how to rob banks" may not be appropriately handed out by judges and policemen. What happens in Colorado and elsewhere points to the activities of destroyers of institutions, among which the military institution is a favored target. But it seems that the military themselves do not know anymore what authority means. If they had an adequate conception of it, they would clarify for themselves the academies' task of preparing students for the defense of, and sacrifice for, the fatherland, and would know how to impose the corresponding convictions and conduct—which does not include a study of pacifism. Instead of accepting the antiauthority mindset, the army ought to be one of the focal points of institutional regeneration. It would then be accused of nurturing an antisocial ideology. But this is still preferable to drifting toward a state of vast disaffection among young people vis-à-vis the army, as was the case until recently to an alarming degree in Germany and is increasingly so elsewhere. This situation may, in turn, lead to the establishment of a professional army, not based on a nationwide call-up to service. Such a system is not new; it was widely practiced before 1789. The armies consisted of a nucleus of the "King's men," the rest were rather forcibly inducted (for example, in the British Navy), or were mercenaries and volunteers. To what extent a professional army identifies itself with the nation is another matter.

(h) Authority and the State

Granted, authority limits the individual will, and when the State acquires full authority by confiscating all individual and intermediate authority the result is intolerable. Such an eventuality cannot, however, argue against the existence of the State and against its necessity rooted in rational human nature. All the arguments used so far for the defense and illustration of authority can be used to demonstrate this truth. Lacking instincts, man is in need of several concentric restraints according to his age, aspirations, inclinations, and roles in society. And, in turn, the institutions which articulate for him these civilizing, educating, and improving restraints are themselves in need of a yet higher and unifying institution—the State—which has then two functions: one is to preserve the specific personality and function of each institution, the other is to watch over the balance between these institutions and the noninstitutionalized forces of civil society. Examples will illuminate these points, although I am aware that in terms of our American heritage the thesis propounded here is controversial.

The end of the last section, dealing with authority in the army, pinpointed the perils arising when agents of the civil society—in that case, a group of pacifists—interfere with the correct course of an institution. In the cited case, the five pacifists distributing leaflets had been arrested and convicted of trespassing and banned from the campus of the Air Force Academy. Later, however, the U.S. Court of Appeals overturned their convictions, saying that certain areas of the Academy, such as the stadium and the chapel, were public and therefore covered by the free speech provisions of the Constitution. We saw how the Academy's officials, intimidated by this all-too-subtle distinction between "areas" of the campus, invited the pacifists into the classroom. The "spirit" of the court decision was obviously contrary to a judicious and prudent separation of two functions, free speech and national defense: it was a decision favoring interference. It may be legitimately asked whether next time another court will tolerate military interference with the rights of free speech.

In the case just mentioned, the civil society interfered with an institution. When unions strike against school boards and paralyze teaching for weeks, at times for months, we have the case of one institution blocking the normal processes of another—even though the personnel of both overlap. Such cases (strikes by certain sectors of public employees, like the subway conductors some years ago in New York City, or recently the San Francisco police) are many times not even legal, yet the State is unable to enforce the law, let alone protect an institution against intolerable pressure and encroachment.

A third illustration may be the series of "investigations" sparkplugged by reporters into the activities of various government agencies dealing with national defense (CIA, FBI, Pentagon) and of the presidency (Watergate). The status of reporters and of the press generally is undefined:

do they form an institution or are they free agents of civil society? A similar question might be asked with regard to labor unions: are they "voluntary private associations," a pressure group of civil society and, thus, what one may call a *feudality,* or are they, collectively, an institution? If the latter, then press and unions would demonstrate it by strictly abiding by the law. Let us say, rather, that newspapers—and, generally, the media—move in that undefined (as yet) area of the public sector where certain groups may have no clear status but enough power to impose their will.[33] In fact, such a group may have no status *because* it is powerful enough not to accept any and to operate according to its own rules. One question is, from where do newspapers and their reporters derive the authority to pursue the highest official and the most important agencies of the State clearly beyond the limits of national interest and of the common good? From the right of the people to be informed? There is no such right; it is invented by the media in order to satisfy their own interests, not those of the public. It is really the right of the media to have the rights they want. While these "rights" may be exercised in criminal cases, it is evident that they should not be allowed to turn indiscriminately against any person and institution. In these areas, too, then, the State is unable to exercise its vested authority. We cannot expect lesser institutions to do any better, that is, to uphold their own authority.

But whence does the State itself derive its authority? Philosophers and jurists have been debating this question throughout history. First of all, they must face the argument that there should be no State at all, a thesis proposed by the anarchists and in an attenuated form by the libertarians. The first hold that small, unstructured groups can govern themselves and conclude pacts with other such groups. The position runs at once into an obstacle: what agency will guarantee the pact and arbitrate in case of aggression (or simply, disagreement) among groups? If there is such an agency, a new pact is required between it and the various groups—and a State comes into existence. The second hold that the State is established by a contract which limits its authority to the preservation of order and property (John Locke). But other libertarians push this logic further: each new generation should start with a new contract; its parents' contract should not bind them. Jefferson was not adverse to this position. Any group, dissatisfied with the contract, exits from the State and, possibly, finds its place in a new one, or indeed initiates a new one. Surveying this progression, the great political writer Otto Gierke noted: "Here the theory of contract touches an extreme where, by denying the will of yesterday any authority over the will of today, it condemns itself to suicide."[34]

The absurdity of the anarchist and libertarian positions, their "self-condemnation to suicide," as Gierke writes, takes us back to firmer

66

ground where we assume, as we did in the case of *all* authority, that the existence of the State is inscribed in human nature. It *is* the condition of self-government because the ideal situation is when, in Gierke's words, neither society nor the individual becomes a means to the other, and their spheres are attuned in concord and harmony. Indeed, the only debate engaged in by Western political thinkers involved not the existence, but the origin and nature of the State: roughly, the medieval theorists argued that the State is a whole with its own personality because every individual, not only the physical but also the moral person (State, corporation, family, and so on) reproduces as a microcosm, the total order, the macrocosm; all of them are creations of God.

This view was compatible with decisive limitations imposed on the State. The Ruler in his law-making and other public functions was subject to the moral law; he also shared his power with the people (Estates) in a sort of dualism, so that the intermediate bodies, as it is implicit in the previous sentence, also had a legal existence. In the medieval mind there was no contradiction between this arrangement and the firm conviction that a common purpose can be effectual only when the One rules over the Many and directs the Many to the common objective (*salus publica*).

Over against this theory, the natural law thinkers led by Jesuits and other Renaissance scholars maintained that the State is rooted in natural law and that between it and the only other natural law product, the family, the local communities and other corporate bodies have but a secondary existence: they were regarded, Gierke writes, "as having arisen only after the constitution of political order; they are useful but not indispensable divisions of the body politic." (p. 63.)

For our discussion of the authority of the State the distinctions made by holders of these two basic positions are useful, even though we believe one can reconcile at least parts of them. Let us observe that the contract theory is not really essential if it is understood that it is *natural* for men to live in a State: a contract contains clauses for the liquidation of a partnership, whereas the well-ordered State contains in itself its own end in view of which the other bodies demarcate their sphere of activity. The State would be a threatening entity only if it were true, as Hobbes assumes, that an abyss separates the state of nature from the social state: then the passage from the former to the latter would be a plunge from absolute freedom into absolute tyranny. But there is for rational human beings no *status naturalis*; this was only assumed when European navigators began meeting "savage" natives whose social and political structures they could not comprehend. They were assumed to live in a "natural state." But man as man always lived in a *status socialis,* that is, under structured authority. Even if one assumes that at one point in history (or prehistory) our ancestors sat down to work out a "contract" of coexistence, one must immediately further assume that they had brought to this solemn occasion quite a bit of political-legal sophistication, acquired from a previous such occasion, and so on, retrogressing to a hypothetical "first occasion." In fact, both contract theorists and natural law theorists are compelled to postulate such a retrogression: Locke argues that even before the establishment of the *status socialis* property at least existed as a result of labor; and Grotius elaborated the theory of "sociability," presumably an intermediate situation between the state of nature and the fully social state.

What remains to be done is to show the superior position of the State vis-à-vis the other social bodies and persons, a superiority on which its authority rests. The contractualists have a rather lame explanation for what is, after all, a fact of experience. They say that not one, but two contracts were passed: one which catapulted men into the establishment of a social state; the second which contractually subordinated these free men to the Ruler. Hobbes further dramatizes the case when he writes that the two contracts were quasi-simultaneous, so that the members of constituted society at once signed away their just-acquired equality in favor of leviathan. When political thinkers say that the State is superior to other social bodies and that it exercises authority over them, they may mean one of two things: some mean, for example Jean Bodin at the end of the sixteenth century, that the intermediate bodies (*collegia et corpora*) enjoy as much freedom as the State grants or tolerates; others, like Althusius (sixteenth and seventeenth century), mean that the provinces and local communities surrender to the State as much of their rights as is required for the purposes of the higher community. The principle of subsidiarity may strike a balance between these positions inasmuch as it does not consider a largely fictitious historical process; it regards it as the basic datum of the human condition that the lower communities (from the individual and the family up to the State) ought to deal with whatever may fall in the field of their competence. This does not imply that they "yield" the rest to higher bodies, but that each of the latter has *its* field of competence. This follows from the order of the world, not from the more or less selfish attitude of the various groups.

The State's authority thus follows from its place in the human and social order. It ultimately guarantees the authority of the other institutions and assists them in their endeavor to serve the common good. Thus, the first servant of the common good is the State itself, but it is obvious that it could not assume this role without the institutions which serve partial goods. The State's function is also educative, it articulates to these institutions the unequal tasks that are theirs in the service of the common good, hence also their unequal positions, spheres of action, and rights. That the object of this educative function ought to be, in the first place, the State itself, is rather evident: it must know what its own limits are in serving the common good, and consequently not usurp the sphere of action of other bodies. This is why I said before that both State and individual (or group) have their own ends which ought not to collide. On the other hand, it is worth noting that the State in all history has been most insistent on possessing the monopoly (or ultimate authority) over three matters: defense, the judiciary, and finances (budget). In other areas its presence was a shared one (education, industry, church, public art, family), according to the contingencies of historical situations.

If we admit that the State possesses the ultimate authority without which other institutions would lack theirs, we understand also that this authority may be threatened or at least challenged by the stronger ones among these institutions and by pressure groups from civil society which gradually acquire a hidden, undeclared power. History shows the almost uninterrupted power struggle through which institutions tend to go beyond their legitimate sphere of influence and action (armies, political parties, churches, feudal bodies, unions, and so on); more modern centuries have witnessed, in addition, the rise of pressure groups in liberal societies which, although they lack institutional structure and establishment, may become tremendous power concentrations. The fact that according to liberal standards of nomenclature they can be labeled as "private, voluntary associations" does not mean that the appetite for power does not come to them as naturally as to any other strong focus of action and influence. Appetite for power is normally an open-ended thrust; when a strong State blocks the horizon, such a pressure group that I am describing is satisfied with limited horizontal expansion, financial success, and intellectual influence; when, as in the case of the modern liberal State, the horizon is not blocked and it appears even inviting, the appetite is vertically directed—not, indeed, to substitute itself for the State, but to acquire first rank within it and usurp its authority in specific areas and on specific issues.

It would have been natural to treat the problem of the media and authority in the section devoted to authority in art and literature. This would have been in my estimation, however, a *lapsus* because the media, whatever their beginnings centuries ago, have since become *mass* media with an immensely swollen influence and power over *mass* society. Thus, the media's role is unquestionably a political one, and as such, it belongs to the section on authority in the State. Today, the media, more than the army, more than any other institution and pressure group, directly challenge, if they do not, indeed, endanger the State's natural authority. In so acting, they no longer need to lean on the public, as in a very real sense union power does not lean on the workers' consensus. Media (and unions) have become independent powers; they decide what the public (a nebulous thing, anyway) should demand and also how the public should react to demands fulfilled or resisted. The media are able, thus, to corner an entire area of public policy and take it out of the government's hands, if not, indeed, its jurisdiction. This is what happened with American involvement in the Indochina war and, the media's appetite being whetted for more power, with other areas of national policy, whether domestic investigations or foreign policy decisions.[35]

This is not the place to analyze media power in depth; in the various American studies of which I know, such a depth-analysis was not attempted because the writers are not yet aware that they deal not with sporadic or even systematic abuse of power, but with the emergence of a *political power* commensurate with the modern combination: mass society and weak State. All I wished to accomplish in this all-too-brief account was to show that the issue of media versus censorship can no longer be discussed as an issue of intellectual freedom versus censorship. The media do not represent intellectual freedom, they represent political power; their curbing is not "censorship" but may well be—soon—a necessary political act.

(i) Authority in Relations Among States

It was held in the Middle Ages that the world ought to have one government because the human race was one. Not even the division between spiritual power (the Church) and the temporal power (Emperor) was regarded as normal, independently of the notorious conflict to which this division had led in the course of the eleventh and twelfth centuries. Later, the already discussed theorists of natural law argued that although the international world is still in a state of nature, that is, without constituted authority recognized by the states as positioned above them, one must postulate a "pre-international" law as binding on individual states as the pre-political law; that is, the natural law was binding upon individual men, compelling them to form societies and states. Yet, even Montesquieu in the eighteenth century accepted the notion that states live vis-à-vis each other in a state of nature:

> Violence, excluded from within the nation [cité] by civil law, continues to persist among nations. There is no written law (there is only religion and natural law) which would regulate the relationship of sovereign governments [princes]. War no longer exists between individuals but it goes on between nations . . . . A sovereign nation which does not live under the authority of civil law . . . may at all times use force or submit to it . . . . Treaties it concludes under duress are as compulsory as those to which it

70

consents . . . and it should not complain that it had to submit to the clauses of a treaty by violence. This would mean that it complains of being in a state of nature . . . as if it wanted to exercise the rights of sovereignty with regard to other sovereigns, as if other sovereigns were its subjects; [such a claim] would go against the nature of things.[36]

In spite of this clearly outlined case that sovereign nations live in a state of nature, the natural law theorists were also correct to argue for the existence of a law which renders international relationships less full of violence than they otherwise could be. There has always been an area created mostly by an unwritten law (charity, fairness, honor, fear) in which restrictions were self-imposed by nations and help was extended to each other's citizens, for example, when they fell prisoners. There are no permanent norms in these relationships, but there are in every age standards of behavior, channels through which affairs are conducted, diplomatic instruments and practices, and institutions serving as clearinghouses. In our century, though, there is a definite regression to earlier states of violence: kidnapping, the taking of hostages, skyjacking, terrorism, and the wide acceptance of partisan fighting with its totally lawless practices.

It is then evident that there is no authority in international relations and that naked interest dictates the behavior of nations in war and in peace. The international bodies themselves behave according to the self-interest of groups of members and have recourse to as much violence as is compatible with their essential weakness. There is no doubt that if they become more powerful, not their moral stance but their proneness to violence would increase. Yet, we must ask, why there is no such thing as an international authority, that is, a world State? There is, after all, a popular argument, according to which it had taken many thousands of years for the moral-social conscience of mankind to reach the degree at which the *status socialis* could come into existence; a certain time will pass until the same moral-social conscience climbs a new step on the evolutionary ladder and issues forth in a world State. Events like the atom-bombing of Japan are believed inevitably to accelerate the process.

It is not hard to see the fallacy of this sort of reasoning. As said before, there has never been a *status naturalis*; it is a fiction of jurists. From the beginning of history, that is, as soon as there were human beings, they lived in communities, under law and authority, with set objectives and observance of the common good. In other words, no time was needed for the State to evolve; it has always been a datum of the human condition. Why is it then, we ask again, that throughout all this time no world State was established, except in the minds of some abstraction-chasing thinkers? We may try to answer with Tocqueville:

71

Man has been created by God in such a way that the larger the object of his love the less directl'y attached is he to it. His heart needs particular passions; he needs limited objects for his attraction to keep these firm and enduring . . . . I am convinced that the interests of the human race are better served by giving every man a particular fatherland than by trying to inflame his passions for the whole of humanity. *(The European Revolution.)*

Let us observe that here a fervent Christian spoke for whom the failure of the medieval *christiana respublica* was well known, as also the doctrine of the unity of the human race. A spiritual unity, Tocqueville would have answered our query in this regard, not a political one.

There is no such thing as an international political authority, precisely because the individual needs communitarian reinforcements (see our discussion in the preceding chapter) in order to conform to his rational social nature. These reinforcements can make sense to him only if they are not of the widest scope, unless they are of a spiritual nature. We understand easily and so does the "primitive" animist and fetishist, too—that we are all children of one God; but it is meaningless for us to be told that we are citizens of the world. We may travel widely, note the similarities among men, and feel sympathetic here to a suffering fellowman, there to a famine-stricken region; but for our active part to be meaningfully invested we need a limited community and a limited objective. I have witnessed several times in my travels the work of missionaries in many parts of the world and the dedication of men and women in various nations on a mission from their governments; their presence was fervently appreciated only because they spent many years, often many decades, serving a particular need (sick care, teaching, the development of a project, a new way of producing food) in a particular area among a given group of people. When he deals outside his political community, a man does not wish to belong to a larger community in order for him to bring forward his social-political qualities; they suffice without an overarching political stimulant.

The second reason for the nonexistence of a world State is that man's self-identification is not given to him as it is given to animals, through external signs and instincts. A rhinoceros will never fall into the error of believing he is an elephant, a cat will never bark, a zebra will not get rid of his stripes. Due to his rationality and the infinite richness of his soul, a man is able to adapt himself to any situation and assume a large variety of behaviors, opinions, loyalties, languages. He is, thus, more in need of marking his separate identity, including his group identity. He adopts symbols to differentiate himself from others across the fence or across the borders. The national flag, the language, the laws, and the mores are ways for him to develop those "particular passions" for "limited objects" (Tocqueville) without which he cannot live except in a state of depression and demoralization, ultimately as a worthlessly drifting figure.

One may counter argue that new developments on a world or even on a cosmic scale will enlarge the field of man's loyalty: he will identify himself with the whole earth, since all mankind is now launched on the conquest of space, a common adventure. Two answers are in order. The global wars and the global bodies like the United Nations have not succeeded in changing the national feeling which, if anything, is stronger and more inward looking today than it was in the so-called "age of nationalism," the nineteenth century. In fact, a new separatist ideology has been added to it, the race consciousness or ethnicity, creating new dividing lines throughout the earth. As far as the "space age" is concerned, it resembles more and more the "age of discovery" when navigators of Spain, Portugal, Italy, England, France, and Holland enlarged in a few decades (1485–1530) the horizon of Western man in every direction and in every respect. Did a common European enterprise arise out of this magnificent venture? Not at all; the navigators, merchants, conquistadors, even the missionaries (see the conflict between Jesuits and Dominicans regarding the Christianization of China) merely carried their home-bred dissensions to the New World and continued battling under different climates.[37]

One cannot speak of authority on a world scale if we mean, as we have mostly done, institutional authority to which individuals and groups obey. Yet, let us have another look at the substance of authority. In every case so far discussed it was clear that authority is order as opposed to disorder, anarchy. Even a gang of murderers obeys one chief because if each acted on his personal impulse, the resulting chaos would thwart their enterprise. Thus, under all circumstances authority is preferable to anarchy. Not only authority as such, but authority exercised which, as we saw, is its essence. Although there is no "world order" in the political sense, there are standards of international conduct which follow from man's moral nature. Such standards have always been operative, but they do not constitute a network of reliable behavior on which a world law might be based. At any rate, the substance of a law would still be lacking because there would be nobody to enforce it. But insofar, precisely, that these standards are not enforced, there is no reason why a great power should not become the agent of these standards and enforce them. This is the only moral, as distinct from political, justification of what we call in this century "imperialism."

Such a stance cannot be erected into law. Suppose, indeed, that great power X, let us say the United States, loses its status, and that great power Z, the Soviet Union, inherits it. The consequence would be a lowering of standards; would we want them to be enforced? Hence the fragility of any international order, also of an international authority merely enforced by a powerful nation. Yet, it is the only screen between some order and none—provided that the nation in question adheres to

73

principles of elementary morality. Otherwise, it would be a totalitarian order, that is, disorder, since men—and nations—may live a human and national life only when they are able to tie the multiple orders, to which they naturally and rationally belong, into a coherent network. Totalitarianism persecutes all the orders and replaces them with its own, whether on a national or an international plane. It is just another label for a permanent civil war in which one antagonist, the quasi-entirety of the nation, is paralyzed. No authority exists under these circumstances, since the restraint exercised over the people is neither rational nor charismatic. In international relations this would translate as a gang of criminals let loose among a multitude.

Notes

1. Karin Judkins, "Towards Zero Birthrate?" *Reader's Digest* (August 1975).
2. *L'Homme contre lui-même* (Paris: Nouv. Editions Latines, 1962), p. 291.
3. The next chapter will discuss the causes of this aversion to authority.
4. It has not been noted that an incalculable harm is done to schoolchildren by teachers' strikes. Through them, the child perceives his teachers as indifferent to teaching, which, in the child's eyes, is a sacred activity. One may wonder if he does not ask himself whether one day his parents will not strike, too.
5. "It is the peculiar characteristic of men and societies . . . that they reserve their most unqualified devotion for those ideals and personalities which they find difficult to realize or emulate." R. Niebuhr, *Does Civilization Need Religion?* (New York: Macmillan, 1927), p. 80.
6. Max Weber spoke of this process as the "bureaucratization of charisma"; after the born leader has set the objective, it is institutionalized by lesser personalities, the bureaucrats of the organization.
7. Younger teachers now in the universities brought their radical ideas, learned in their classes during the 1960s, to the curriculum. Through the authority shift, they are able to impose these ideas. The resulting situation is evident in all courses. In history departments, for example, "narrative history" is frowned upon, students are told to "make up their own minds" from material collected by them, and to discuss fashionable issues, such as "the racism of Abraham Lincoln." As a commentator has put it, not only is the student's attention directed to irrelevant issues, the method itself discourages the formation of a historical sense, the sense of the pastness of the past or of the irreducible quality of time.
8. In the university where I teach, it has become a regular practice that each time students oppose a decision by the president, they gather under his office windows, chanting: "——— is a liar!" The effect of this ceremonialized disrespect is incalculably demoralizing since no sanctions are ever taken, no attempt is made to disperse the group, let alone penalize its members.
9. A little informal survey I made in my classes at Brooklyn College indicated, alas, that all twenty-eight students enthusiastically approved the new California curriculum—in the name of the individual's right to choose his course of studies. It occurred to none that the California program, too, was after all an imposed one, and, on the better students, a cruelly imposed one at that.
10. *On Authority and Revelation* (New York: Harper, 1966), p. xv
11. Kierkegaard himself, preoccupied with the problem of divine authority, put in the center of his religious thought the case of Abraham, ready to sacrifice his son on the authority of the sole voice of God—against reason, paternal love, and the knowledge that he can have no other offspring.
12. *Chrétiens sans Eglise* (Paris: Gallimard, 1969).
13. A sentence by the Kant-follower Forberg (end of the eighteenth century)

summarizes well the concept of the self-idolator: "Anyone who sees the deity outside of himself in the flux of things will never find that deity." Quoted in C. Fabro, *God in Exile* (Westminster, Md.: Newman Press, 1968), p. 519.

14. *Tradition and Authority*, p. 61.

15. One can also train inmates in a concentration camp to develop habits. This is, however, counteracted by a permanent inner revolt, since neither is the initial consent secured nor can one see afterward the good of the habit.

16. *An Essay on the Development of Christian Doctrine* (New York: Doubleday, 1960), p. 201.

17. Rolf Dahrendorf, *Class and Conflict in Industrial Society* (Stanford, Calif.: Stanford University Press, 1959), p. 168.

weakened by the weakening of the penal system. The church is not a social agency and it is only indirectly a civilizing force, the consequence of turning men toward their salvation.

20. This is hardest to achieve with the family where biological and elementary-psychological functions render the parents indispensable and their authority established already by the time the child reaches five or six years of age. This hard-core resistance of the family to the confiscation of its mediating role makes it the target of unceasing efforts to abolish or at least dilute it. Totalitarian regimes, utopian blueprints, and progressive educators try, in various ways, to remove children from the family circle; to weaken parental ties by preaching free love or abortion; to make children question parental authority (via questionnaires distributed in class where the child is supposed to classify and rate his parents); to put doubt in parents' minds about their competence and authority in matters of education. Other institutions, more open to public scrutiny and control, are less able to protect themselves against the trend.

21. The Mexican land-reform system is a case in point. The beneficiaries (*egidarios*) are not authorized to sell their plots; nevertheless, they find ways of doing so; the result is that land accumulates in the hands of the hard-working, the prosperous, the influential, who may even hire as a farmhand or tenant the official owners of some of his land.

22. This analysis does not include the case of economic "self-determination" where a group of people, preferably small, jointly exploit an economic venture (cooperative). Here authority can indeed be divided into equal parts, although it is doubtful whether such an enterprise can last. The division of functions tends to create inequalities.

23. I realize that in such cases the enterprise may be said to operate at a (economic) loss, made up by other parts of society in form of open or hidden subsidy. Yet, this in itself proves that profit is not an essential objective for all enterprises.

24. Seen from the vantage point of our habits engendered by our thoroughly industrialized society, it is hard even to imagine life in countries not yet industrialized, at least to the same degree. Spain is a good example of the latter. Holidays, saints' days, local fiestas lasting for several days, family celebrations, and so on, have at least as great an impact on the course of life as work and efficiency-mindedness. Next to work rhythm there is also a leisure rhythm, not in the sense of "rest from work" but as a form of the outlook on existence.

25. *The Ancien Régime* (New York: Harper, 1974), I., p. 212.

26. Let us note, though, that Socrates, arguing along lines similar to ours, accepted the *intellectually* unjust penalty as *socio-politically* justified.

27. We are speaking of realities rather than of "values." But truth becomes a "value" seen from the angle of community.

28. The man sentenced to be executed is regarded also as a sacred figure: his last wish is done as a propitiating sacrifice on the altar of the dead.

29. The soul is not merely rational, which does not mean antirational or irrational. For example, when we are "transported" (a significant term) by music or seek expression through symbols (which characterizes the medieval mind), the nonrational faculties of the soul come into evidence.

30. Even "official" psychology begins to admit this much, when some psychologists argue that to counter our selfish biological impulses, societies evolve ethical and religious rules favoring the group over the individual. (See the address to the American Psychological Association [September 1975] by its president, Donald T. Campbell.)

31. That it cannot deny the necessity of protecting society is obvious. But I insist that it cannot deny the validity of punishment either: in other words, a purely rehabilitative court would turn into a hospital—and by the same token would no longer protect society from criminals. We are now witnessing the victory of this concept.

32. September 1975 issue of *Forewarned*, a publication of the Public Service Research Council.

33. See on the subject of the media the end of this section.

34. *Natural Law and the Theory of Society* (Boston: Beacon Press, 1960), p. 110.

35. Many internationally known authorities have pointed out that the responsibility for the Vietnam debacle rested, to an extent out of all proportion, on a few reporters from the American press and television. The leader of the Khmer Rouge, at his first press conference in Phnom Penh publicly thanked the *New York Times'* correspondent for the aid extended by "progressive-minded" Americans to communist victory. The correspondent did not refuse these words of gratitude, although offensive and humiliating to the American government whose secondary position was, thus, underlined by the Khmer Rouge representative; the latter practically implied that the real government of America is the *New York Times*. Seymour Hersh, another *Times* reporter, seems to have made a specialty of attacking American defense institutions and America's allies when the latter do not fit Hersh's ideological preferences. After his anti-CIA campaign, this reporter turned his venom on Chile. After a while, he admitted that he had been hoping to find incriminating evidence on the CIA's role in bringing down the Allende regime and to help a right-wing regime come into power. This would have been a good story to write about, he said, but since in spite of his fervent efforts he found nothing, he decided that there was "no story." In other words, only such stories are "good stories" which harm the United States government or its allies.

36. *The Spirit of the Laws*, Book XXVI, Chapter 20.

37. The argument that the establishment of the United States is proof that in the age of discovery or as its consequence the various European nations were able to set up a *united* aggregate of nationalities, races, creeds, and so on, is not a valid one. By definition, all immigrants uprooted themselves; and not as nationals but as displaced persons—in fact, isolated individuals—did they found a new entity.

4.
The Enemies of Authority

Before turning our attention to the motives of those who oppose authority, it might be useful to state the essentials we found about authority itself. The opponents usually speak of "authoritarianism" and call themselves "antiauthoritarians," showing thereby that they have fashioned a straw man and around it an ideology. An "authoritarian" would be, it seems to me, a man who makes a fetish of a certain attitude which we mean when we say "he throws around his weight," a man whose every manifestation oozes orders and commands. If we try to visualize him, we think of a firm-jawed, strong man, with severe eyes and stony features, unbending to human motivations, inscrutable, unapproachable, and ruthless. This picture, modeled after the antifascists' caricature of Mussolini, is not only false, it is also childish, because it is superficial and biased. "Authoritarianism" is a monolithic stance worthy to be satirized by a Charlie Chaplin movie; authority, in contrast, is the rational mode of structuring a human community, society's self-protection against chaos. More than that, authority is not only a social instrument, it also corresponds to the individual's need for rational action, to his comprehension of the place that is his in the various orders to which he belongs and which intersect.

The rationality of the exercise of authority must be carefully stressed because, as we shall see, its opponents have a rather different notion of rationality, hence of man himself. They do not speak of the human being as he is or as he could be if he followed the traditional moral injunctions; they prefer to argue as if the object of discourse were not the human being but a utopian pseudo-ideal, a kind of "autonomous man," self-sufficient and mechanically positive—according to the value system of authority's enemies. Man as we know him, the man you and I are, is so free of instincts that with almost every step he threatens the very community without which he could not exist and survive as a human being. Thus authority—this is its first function—mediates between man's two basic needs: to be free and to be integrated with the group, and it mediates rationally because it is rational for man to live in the community of other men. If human groups are always precarious and precariously balanced between order and anarchy, it is because man is a place of conflict between his rational desire to be free and his equally rational desire to belong to the group. The second function of authority is that of structuring inequality. Without it, human groups would be worse than the proverbial "unruly herd," since an animal herd is never unruly; it obeys, often even in a stampede, signals from its leaders. In a human group, all the inventions of a free will may be used against each other—if the group is not structured according to natural and artificial lines of inequality, of superior and inferior abilities, roles, incomes, responsibilities, positions, competences, and so on.

The third function of authority implies more than structuring and ordering a community: through the use of reason in the service of an objective we perceive a higher law than the one in the name of which we obey the given authority. Authority tends to a good and it trains us in the habit of envisaging it. The child who obeys parental authority understands in the course of time something about the nature of the laws operating in his community, hence about the nature of man as a rational being. This is why I wrote earlier that authority is educative in more than one respect.

Let us now endeavor to enter the world of the opponents of authority. We are likely to meet them today among psychologists, psychiatrists, and progressivist ideologues whom I prefer to call "utopians."[1] Much of their own authority (and authoritarian, intolerant declarations) is derived from the self-built and now hardly challenged pedestal from which they propose the following diagnosis of man and community: the misery of this age takes its cause from the rightist regimes in power in Europe between 1920 and 1945. These were totalitarian regimes, successful because they gave a political expression to a dangerous streak in the upbringing of generations according to traditional authoritarian methods. The tendency toward the progressive emancipation of mankind, begun with the age of enlightenment, was thus blocked. Men and women accustomed at home to submit to the father found it again convenient, as in the dark ages, to take refuge in these newly chaotic times (war, revolutions, depression) under the protection of a father figure, a leader, a big brother. Frightened by insecurity around them, they had no desire to oppose such a man; they executed his will uncritically and in a spirit of subservience. (It will be remembered that there were American psychologists in the 1950s who "explained" the Russian people's submission to Stalin's rule as the result of the custom of swathing babies. The Russians, accustomed from tender age not to use their bodies and limbs freely, were said to be easily submissive to authority. The problem is, what do we make of the case of Solzhenitsyn and other Russian dissidents, intrepid critics, and opponents of the regime?) The same theme, with variations, has been used by psychologists and educationists in this country, applied to local circumstances. Men like John Dewey and Dr. Spock could argue that while in the United States there had been no "authoritarian" regimes, the puritanic ethos was nevertheless based on blind authority and a certain curtailment of the freedom of self-expression.

The case having been so made, the prophylactic measures are assumed to be evident. If we reduce and erode authority in its chief manifestations: father, teacher, priest, judge, army officer, head of state, and so on, then the "new man," the antiauthoritarians argued in essence, will learn to be defiant of authority, democratically minded, cooperative, tolerant, and free. The removal of authority in family, classroom, army, and civic life will liberate man from age-old bondage and allow his true self, an autonomous yet cooperative self, to emerge from the fetters of tradition. This is the condition of reorganizing society, indeed mankind, on happier foundations. A French reviewer of Professor Stanley Milgram's book, *Obedience to Authority,* to which we shall turn our attention in a moment, went so far as to assert in praise of the book that "always and everywhere the condition of freedom is an attitude of general and systematic scepticism vis-à-vis the principles that authority wishes to impose."[2]

This line of argumentation must be called ideological because it fastens upon a certain interpretation of current history (by no means adequate), then extrapolates this interpretation so as to validate it for the nature of man (the second unwarranted conclusion). Hence my previous warning of the advisability to question this view of human nature and particularly this view of rational behavior, which is here reduced to a rejection of authority as the key to paradise. Conversely, this view typically equates irrationality (the alienation of one's autonomy and personhood) with the acceptance of authority, a manifest contradiction to the structuring function of authority. It would then follow that life in an ordered society is ipso facto irrational, and that the "good society" is one in which everybody pursues his own desires autonomously, that is, he gives the law to himself. Indeed, this is what the earlier mentioned French reviewer of Milgram's book, M. Roland Jaccard, actually suggests: "The moment that an individual renounces his moral code so as to become an integral part of society's structured hierarchies, he sheds his humanity."

The blatant nonsense of this view surfaces already in the "progressive" family where the child takes all the freedom he wishes—but himself becomes an "authoritarian" figure since the family submits to his whims. The same thing would happen in the "progressive" community also, where some would finally arrogate more power to themselves than what is theoretically theirs when everybody is "autonomous"; they would impose their tyranny on a truly submissive, fearful mass of unstructured people. In fact, this is what happens in communes in California. Runaway youth who join communes become will-less tools of the leader. The latter appoints an assistant who remains with the new recruit day and night, never leaves him or her alone, they share meals, blankets, stealing and foraging activities. Note that like in other utopian communes known from history, here, too, the member has no individual property (he must divest himself of whatever he could bring or steal from home), and has to marry the person appointed by the leader—unless the commune advocates free love.

The present antiauthority theories are then mostly ideologically motivated; this is evident also from the fact that the word "authority" is used only to describe traditional forms of authority—in family, church, courts, army—and right-wing political regimes, but never left-wing movements and regimes even if they are totalitarian. The explanation is not far to find: the opponents of authority who are, together with their disciples, influential today, Horkheimer, Adorno, Fromm, Erikson, and others, were in the 1920s believers in leftist, including Soviet, "experiments," and had committed themselves to the thesis that the "old society" was repressive and that the "new society" will emancipate all mankind. Their hopes and emotions fueled the groups which have been applauding for half a century now the progress of destruction of traditional structures and the conquests by leftist, revolutionary ideology. Even when the latter deviated from the hoped-for course of universal emancipation and set up new and terrible despotisms, the label of "authoritarianism" was not applied to them.

While the trends opposed to authority are ideological and quite often outright political, the roots of opposition can be detected at deeper levels. We shall examine two cases in which antiauthority themes intermingle and give us an adequate panorama of the problem. The political motivation is not absent from these cases simply because authority—and its negation—stands centrally embedded in community life. One may even say that the principal issue upon which authority and its enemies center is the definition of *political man.*

(a) The Frankfurt School

The so-called Frankfurt School (of sociological research) which, in the late 1930s, transferred its activities from Germany to the United States— first to New York's Columbia University, then to California—focused its attention, among other investigations, on the "authoritarian personality." A book by the same title has been for decades the leading source for the study of the problem; its authors and readers thought they had finally understood the psychological and sociological mechanisms of tension, conflict, and war, the hidden motivations of the type of men who initiate aggression and escalate tense situations into violence and war. The study claimed to be scientific, although its credentials were more than doubtful. With the autonomous man as their ideal (not a scientifically warranted one, but a mere dream), they had to explain why it was that after the age of enlightenment and Marx, now that the industrial society was finally a rationally organized one, the first such in history, the world was still producing in abundance authoritarian personalities, leaders and follow-ers. One of the main features of the book was the so-called F scale, measuring authoritarian personality traits which, when summarized, pro-duced the portrait of the authoritarian character: a mechanical surrender to conventional values; blind submission to authority, together with blind hatred of all opponents and outsiders; hostility to introspection; rigid, stereotyped thinking; a penchant for superstition; half-moralistic, half-cynical vilification of human nature. The attitude scale was so designed as to uncover and quantify estimates of anti-Semitism, ethnocentrism, eco-nomic conservatism, and so on.

In consequence, not only did the Frankfurt School have a built-in ideo-logical bias vis-à-vis the "authoritarian personality," not only did it con-struct a straw man with the help of a supposedly scientific questionnaire, it also completely misjudged the function of authority, which it equated with negative traits like "blind," "mechanical," "conventional," "su-perstitious," "rigid," "cynical," and so on. In a way, and with consider-able naiveté, the supposedly sophisticated authors, the prestigious Theo-dore Adorno and his colleagues, unmasked their own portraits, which became embarrassingly transparent through their adjectives. Yet, such was the Frankfurt School's ambition to refashion society and make it safe against the recurrence of policies and regimes like the ones in the 1930s, that the directors and collaborators of the institute attempted to construct a whole science around their own basic ideological commitment, the so-called "critical theory." The curtain fall was appropriately inglorious and had almost the value of a refutation of what the Frankfurt School had set out to achieve. When Professor Adorno, one of the two celebrated directors—with Horkheimer—of the School, began lecturing to students one day in 1970 in Frankfurt (the School had resettled after the war in its place of origin), women students surrounded his lectern, bared their bosoms, and attacked him for being an agent of American imperialism. A few weeks later Adorno died of a heart failure, probably in utter incomprehension of the fact that his theories had been turned upon him with a vengeance. After the bared bosom incident he did indeed declare to the journalists: "When I was teaching my critical theory I did not imagine that the students would turn it into Molotov cocktails."

Yet, one does not have to be a critical theorist to interpret correctly what happened: authority is so much a part of man's makeup that he expects it to be exercised and is frustrated when it is not forthcoming from the appropriate sources. Why did the students turn against Adorno, and generally against their liberal-progressivist professors in America as well as in Europe? For two interlocking reasons. One was that they knew that from these men no answer can be expected to the questions of existence with which all serious human science ultimately deals. By denying authority not only to the life of the community, but also to reality itself, these professors, locked in their subjectivity, in their *self,* grievously damaged the students' relationship with what *is,* blocking not only their quest for community, but also their quest for being and truth. In fact, they were teaching them that to look for answers is the intellectual equivalent of looking for authority, for the father figure, and that to look for community was the equivalent of submitting to an authoritarian regime. But there is not the slightest doubt that these young people *are* looking for answers, not just for any, but for true answers. Yet, their professors inhibited this aspiration, intellectually and morally; they created an environment in which the student was embarrassed—and more: publicly shamed—if he as much as raised the ultimate problems. The year 1968 and its sequels represented an opportunity for the students to hit back against the merchants of falsehoods, their liberal, antiauthority professors.

The second reason was that the professors (what happened to Adorno is merely one of the many typical cases) did not deliver what they had promised. For years, for decades, they had verbally prepared the heavenly kingdom of the autonomous man, a figure which not only remained obstinately distant, but was liquidated, refuted, denied by the professors' real attitude. The latter preached against authority, yet acted like petty tyrants, thus appearing as agents of the repressive bourgeois society and

State. They seemed, in fact, to be double agents: of the capitalist order, with their salaries, academic and other distinctions, way of life, titles, easy work conditions—and agents at the same time of the revolution they claimed to prepare for. This intellectual double-dealing was resented by a generation of students who took the imminence of the revolution for granted and expected their antiauthority professors to lead them out of the classroom and onto the barricades.

Thus the phenomenon described arose from several causes, but one which is unmistakable is the systematic misuse and abuse of authority. The tragic thing is that even after the events of 1968–70 all the elements of the situation have remained exactly as before: the opponents of authority in positions of a misused authority, and, facing them, the inarticulated mass of students which continue to be led towards the unattainable dream, indeed nightmare, of the autonomous man.

(b) Milgram's Experiment

The second case worth examining is expounded in a recent book describing an experiment of Professor Stanley Milgram.[3] Briefly, Milgram asked his volunteer testers, hired among students and intellectuals (a significant selection), to inflict a certain degree of pain in the form of electric shock on "learners," in reality, not volunteer recruits but Milgram's own assistants, who were supposed to be "punished" each time they gave wrong responses to a sham questionnaire. The "testers" (whose reaction was in fact the object of the experiment, although they did not know it) knew only that the "learners' " pain grew in proportion as the electric shock increased in voltage from tolerable (15 volts) to intolerable (450 volts). What Milgram wanted to find out was how far the testers would obey a laboratory technician—impassive, and clad in gray for more scientific neutrality—in inflicting pain they knew became gradually more unpleasant. Milgram formulated his quest by asking "when and how will people [that is, the testers] defy authority in the face of a clear moral imperative," namely the refusal to continue the torture.

The great majority of the volunteer testers showed their willingness to inflict great pain, a result which greatly shocked Milgram himself as well as the commentators who knew of his experiment or read his account. His own wife called him a "real Eichmann" for devising the experiment itself. In other words, Milgram and his friendly and adverse critics were suddenly shocked out of their comfortable illusion about the nature of man and the unique relationship he maintains with the fact of authority. They were obviously also upset in their pacifist ideology, since Milgram's book showed—contrary to their expectations or at least to their ideals—

that if volunteer testers, many of them students of Yale University, were willing to inflict pain because they were so commanded in the name of a scientific experiment, then soldiers in an army do not have to be inhuman monsters for doing the same when ordered by a considerably stricter source of command and for the defense of their country. After all, the students would not have risked court-martial and execution had they stood up from the laboratory bench and walked out.

What interests us here, however, is not the conclusion Professor Milgram drew from his interestingly devised experiment, but the premises which had gone into the conception of it. In the case of the Frankfurt School, the premise of the authors of the *Authoritarian Personality* was that right-wing regimes cannot be rationally and historically motivated; they are artificially constructed by primitive men with primitive character traits: superstition, hatred, hostility, rigidly stereotyped ideals and attachments.

In the case of Milgram's experience, and the book *Obedience to Authority,* the premises seem to have been the following:

(1) Authority means the infliction of punishment (whether pain or some other form of victimization, physical, moral, psychological) and a certain consent or even pleasure in the act of inflicting punishment—since the act was not interrupted by the agents.

(2) "Authority" is contrasted with what Milgram calls "inner moral qualities"; thus, it is a purely negative, externally induced, immoral attitude. Milgram does not assume that the person exercising authority may do so by moral motives for the good of those who obey his authority. If we think back again to Horkheimer's and Adorno's "portrait of the authoritarian man," we find the same prejudice at work.

(3) Obedience to authority brings about the surrender of one's moral autonomy to another, the source of authority. In other words, the fact that B obeys A implies that to the same extent B ceases to be an integral human being, he must act under duress, paralysis of the will, humiliation, and abject renunciation of his own self.

(4) Authority can only be negative, a flow of evil from the issuer of order to the receiver. It cannot command moral action and lead to something positive or good. Here Milgram simply forgot that when he expects a show of "inner moral qualities" on the part of his volunteer testers, such inner moral qualities are not found incorporated in his imaginary "autonomous man"; they are themselves the products of inculcation by moral *authority*. In other words, Milgram does not even think of granting to authority at least the neutrality we attribute to a knife with which the assassin commits murder and the surgeon performs the act of healing. In his estimation, authority can only be punishing, pain inflicting, a demolisher of moral autonomy.

The assumption which underlies these four interlocking premises is that there is somewhere, or at least that somewhere some time there should be created, an *autonomous man,* unsullied by history and its heavy burden, innocent of tradition, injustice, greed, and intolerance—indeed, of the moral law as hitherto propounded, that is, a law proclaimed *by* God, given *to* men, accepted as an *external* command. If the psychologist, Milgram himself, could reach this deep layer of purity and devise adequate means to render it conscious and active, society would become rational, humane, and cooperative. Yet, when we study the phenomenon of authority, we find, over against this dream image of the autonomous man, a rational being whose rational nature causes him to obey authority. Obey it not blindly, not with the automatism of a robot, but because he is conscious of reason's requirement that he should be integrated with society and take his place in a structured whole which in many ways transcends him. Psychologist Erik Erikson regards the problem of "authoritarianism" as the longing for "totalism" in which he detects the myth of only one kind of man, Aryan man. No doubt, and there are also several studies of Mircea Eliade pointing it out, that all men, not only the Aryan, long for inclusion in larger entities of a spiritual nature, since they are aware of their "selfishness, selfness, and separateness," as we put it on the previous pages. The already quoted Dr. Campbell says it, too (A.P.A. presidential address, Chicago, September 1975) when he perceives "a biological bias in favor of self-seeking, uninhibited behavior," checked by the strong ethical and religious rules which favor the group over the individual. "Love thy neighbor" and "honor thy parents," he said in his speech, serve as brakes on too much antisocial behavior; they balance out the biological bias in the opposite direction. Yet, the views of psychologists Campbell, Erikson, and Milgram need to be further corrected.

When Erikson and even the more comprehending Campbell speak of authority, they mean something that flows from antirational or at least irrational sources: in the first case, from a drive towards totality, in the second case, from a biological substructure. Campbell accepts the theory that all human social behavior has a genetic origin, consequently that both selfishness and its social balance, the group feeling, are biologically determined. Erikson looks at myth—and Campbell looks at biology—as constituting one half of social motivation, the irrational half: if authority issues from this irrational half and is only nature's secret device to integrate the otherwise centrifugally programmed members of society, then human beings submit to authority, because, in the best case, they rationalize its intrusion into their selfish, pleasure-seeking, existence. In this way, however, we merely turn authority into an evil, although a necessary evil, and we are still looking for the autonomous man as the ideal, no longer divided between self and community, between the rational and the irrational.

Milgram's opposition to authority is more radical and more primitive; in fact, despite his carefully set up experiment, he cannot comprehend the phenomenon at all. He seems to hold that if at some point B yields his moral authority to A (B obeys A), what intervene are not "genetic mutations modifying neural networks, hormone distributions, and finally behavior," as Campbell theorizes, but the lingering tradition of past societies which treated man as a child and assumed coercive power over him in the name of invented divine forces. Now, however, in the enlightened age of the twentieth century, science and democracy have dispelled these false beliefs and abolished the submissive behavior resulting from them. Authoritarian people, together with those who obey them, can be only remnants, atavistic survivals, bound to die out sooner or later.

The discussion of the Frankfurt School and of Stanley Milgram's book has given us two illustrations of antiauthority thought. They exemplify the type of opposition to authority and show, at the same time, the kind of fear that the presence of authority at any level of society releases among its critics. The latter turn into all-suspecting sleuths in their vigilance to unmask authority, and we find them, indeed, among the abolitionists of authority and of structured existence in family, church, school, private organizations, army, and the State itself. It may seem strange that they are, simultaneously, fervent partisans of an international authority, of the United Nations, of ecumenism among churches, and so on. In reality, there is no contradiction here. Let us remember Tocqueville's wise observation about man's preference for limited loyalties. Man best functions in such a context; he needs private property, private virtues, symbols of a limited community with which to identify himself. When he is lifted from these natural limits, his loyalties do not proportionately widen, they are deprived of a vitalizing sap. When Eliade speaks of the "longing for totality," this is not to be understood as earthly (horizontal), but as spiritual (vertical): we long to be part of the whole from which we feel we were torn, the whole of transcendant reality, our metaphysical roots. This has nothing to do with membership in an international leviathan in which individuals and also communities lose their identity and give up their struggle for distinguishing symbols of their existence. This is, however, the objective of the opponents of authority: one can no more radically abolish tradition, its network, its structure, than by dissolving it in an anonymous and arid "world community" where tradition would cease playing precisely that function which makes it a living influence in one's life: the function of separating one group from other groups—not in an arbitrary fashion, but because groups themselves are like persons with a definite physiognomy, dimensions, history, and need of precise self-identification. Those who oppose authority know very well that a mere theoretical battle against it achieves no results; but the dissolution of limited communities is more than a good beginning, it deprives the individual of identity and social articulation, thus, of his past and of the sustaining symbols which convey it to him.

How do the enemies of authority proceed in their task? First, by attributing to the exercise of authority, to the climate created by authority, all the negative features to which people generally react with disapproval and condemnation. Secondly, by dissolving the natural communities so as to confuse their members about their own roles and to leave these roles to new, artificial authorities in charge of restructuring the communities and the individuals therein. The so confused groups become like animal herds transported to new grounds, obedient to new leaders. In the case of human communities, the transplantation aims at the psychological and spiritual identity, so that obedience to the new sources of authority becomes resigned, listless, and mechanical. This happened when African blacks were transported to the New World, uprooted men and women without a tribal, family, and personal identity; and it happens now in Cambodia where the communist Khmer Rouge not only drove out two million inhabitants from Phnom Penh, dispersing them in the countryside, but they compulsorily renamed them (!) so that families might not find each other and restore a modicum of ties. A "renamed" person, especially a child, is lifted out of all the sustaining relationships which identify him beyond his bare personality and becomes a mere unit, subservient and pliable, under the whip of the slave master or the communist cadre. We no longer speak then of "authority," only of sheer overpowering force.

What negative features are ascribed to authority by its enemies? According to them, authority is spawned, and in turn engenders and perpetuates, prejudices, introversion, resentment, hatred, inferiority feelings, a preference for rigid forms of discipline, delight in uniforms, mechanical movements, inclination to use and unresistingly accept physical violence, orders given and received. Some of these are the character traits of the Frankfurt School's scale, and they figure also in J.-P. Sartre's famous short story, the "Childhood of a Leader" (L'Enfance d'un Chef), which narrates the early years of a budding fascist boss. A perusal of the lurid display of paperback books in any drugstore offers another sample of supposedly Nazi stories: sex, violence, brutality, an abundance of leather (whips, boots, shoulder straps, coats, belts, blazers), and metal (brass buttons, nails, belt buckles, cartridge boxes), symbols of harshness and physical brutality. The line of quick association of ideas we are supposed to follow subliminally is that authority begins with resentment against the open society where X did not succeed, his gradual turn to authority which dresses him in the garb of vicarious success (the uniform), and finally his degeneracy into brutish violence and right-wing posturing. The strange thing one could observe since 1968 is that not right-wingers but leftists (commandos, terror gangs, kidnappers, liberation armies) have been putting on a quasi-uniform decked out with leather and metal, have adopted violence as a method of breaking up society, and have bowed to authoritarian and totalitarian rulers and aspirant rulers like Mao Tse-tung and Ché Guevara. The fact that many opinion leaders call them "leftist fascists" does not change but rather confirms the suspicion that on Horkheimer's and Milgram's scales authority is condemned only when it is not *their* favorite authority. This seminal prejudice invalidates their core conviction, together with the field and scope of their experiments and the conclusions drawn therefrom. No serious mind, unfettered by their time- and circumstance-bound theories, can do anything but dismiss the whole enterprise.

This does not mean that the enterprise and the vast influence it exercises are not dangerous, that it does not act as a dissolvent of the natural communities and institutions discussed in the last chapter. Let us bear in mind that on their scale of values "authority" stands for traditional morality and society whose persistence blocks the establishment of the ideal society of autonomous men. A child brought up under parent's and teacher's authority becomes, in this view, a willing subject of an "authoritarian" ruler who, in turn, stresses an inward-looking, national tradition and makes use of symbols glorifying one tradition to the exclusion of, and hostility to, the others. If, on the other hand, authority is successfully combated in all national communities—for example, by promoting internationalism and world government—the individual, emancipated from the shackles of groups closer to him such as family, institutions, nation, and church, will be correspondingly more autonomous. He will not only question the authority of others, he will refuse to belong to "closed groups," including, particularly, the closed group called his nation. He will be a cosmopolite, but before reaching that stage, he will have had no habit-forming training in the kind of relationships that authority establishes in the life of communities. The antiauthority militants call such an individual "independent," "nonprejudiced," "open-minded," "liberal," and "tolerant"; in reality, he is unstable, lonely, alienated, unreliable, confused—so atomized in his functions in society that he easily becomes an agent of destruction, a social antibody. Let us assume, however, that he does not have the determination to play actively such a role; then his human inclination to obey authority—which cannot be uprooted in him, only distorted in its growth—will turn him into an easily housebroken member of unnatural and antisocial groups, victim of a descending series of usurped authorities.

This is how hippies, freaks, members of "families," cop-outs, terror organizations, and all sorts of other marginals are fashioned, as also militants of more directly destructive organizations: nihilists, gang members, killers for pleasure, the Manson family or the Baader-Meinhof band. It is fashionable to state of all these people that they had deliberately opted out of society, which bears the ultimate responsibility for their behavior. This is true in one sense only: they are the products of the enemies of authority who reduced them—in family, school, army, and so on—from their human, that is social and rational, status to self-operating units ready to obey the first command which justifies their released antisocial and antirational drives. Such people, victims, to be sure, but not of *society,* only of society's antiauthority subverters, display better than any ingenious experiment could do the selfish, self-centered, separatist nature which is one side of our nature, but which is happily curbed by the cooperation of authorities in various groups. They should be seen not as heralds of the "autonomous man," but as living refutations of antiauthority theories.

Hippies, "families," and so on, are by-products of the antiauthority ideology; the main objective of this ideology is the creation of a world society whose members are structureless individuals, arbitrarily shuffled atoms whose sole identity is their belonging to the frontierless continuum. In communist societies, which in many respects prefigure the utopia to which authority's opponents want to lead mankind, the enterprise is openly practiced. A witness, Bishop Seitz of the Vietnamese city Kontum, described tersely what he saw in 1975, prior to his expulsion (August 15):

> What happens in Cambodia [he said to the newspaper *Le Figaro* August 27, 1975] is only the methodical and radical application of integral Maoism: the building of a new man in a new society. . . . Once the family and village structures are destroyed, namely through mass deportation, the individual becomes an easily maleable material at the hands of the all-powerful party organization. . . . Displaced and dispersed over hundreds of miles, members of a village lose the sense of individual property and can easily become mere working tools of the collectivity.

We have here not only the dissolution of natural communities, mentioned before, but also the formation of new, artificial authorities, despotic because, contrary to our criteria, they do not respond to man's rational aspirations and do not mediate a higher law for him. The objective in the service of which he is enrolled is neither rationally comprehensible, nor does it serve a loyalty-eliciting common good. Let us read further what Bishop Seitz, interviewed on radio channel Europe I, had to say:

> Every individual, from age four till the day he dies, is organized into groups. Children from four to twelve years of age are in the charge of a

woman-commissar; from twelve to sixteen they form a separate group, again from seventeen to twenty-five, then the adults in full force, the aging ones, the oldsters. All, men, women, and children, undergo daily indoctrination in their respective groups.

Needless to say, these groups are the opposite of natural communities and their cohesion is not assured by organically evolving social networks; the members are held together by the fear of being spied on and penalized for nonconformist thought and acts. The official group is also the only one to which each belongs; there is no plurality of groups where freedom might be asserted at the intersecting points. "Authority" consists of the sum of all the fears and punishments each suffers or witnesses the others suffer; the supreme "authority" is not a transcendent being who would be the cause of Milgram's "inner moral qualities," but a human being, the ultimate source of all fears and rewards. Again in Bishop Seitz's words:

> The group of four-year-old children is asked if they want candy and cake. Upon their affirmative answer, they are told to pray for it. The children recite the Pater or the Ave Maria. After a short pause, they are asked: Did you receive what you prayed for? No, we did not, the children answer. Then let us pray to Ho Chi Minh, the leader suggests. The children obey, and, lo and behold, the leader distributes the awaited candy.[4]

* * *

Now that we have the key of the antiauthority ideology, the destruction of authority and its replacement by anarchy, itself leading to naked power over depotentiated and destructured individuals, we can observe how the ideologues practice their creed. The objective is well stated by Yves Simon: "Following Rousseau, the totalitarian State [the institutionalization of the General Will] pursues the destruction of every social group within the State, so as to establish an absolute domination over a crowd of individuals no longer protected by autonomic organizations."[5] I do not wish to suggest that every opponent of authority aims consciously at the establishment of a totalitarian system, but I am convinced that such a system is by necessity found at the end of his logic, whether he pursues it or not. It cannot be denied, however, that the conscious part of his endeavor, a consequence which he could perceive with a little self-criticism, is the fragmentation of authority among an infinity of groups, each claiming full legitimacy over the rest, over the State itself. This quasi-civil strife situation normally leads to the emergence of naked power, whose ambition is then not the reordering of these groups according to their natural functions (this would require their consolidation into larger communities), but quite simply their suppression.

This fragmentation of authority—setting the child against the family, the soldier against his officer, the student against his teacher, the citizen against the State—is the exact opposite of authority as it exists in natural groups. In natural communities authority functions in view of the common good; authority's fragmentation signals the rapid emergence in rather quick succession of socially not matured ad hoc groups which, however, claim immediately full power and are contemptuous of any integration with the common good. Paul Ricoeur calls them "wild groups" (*groupes sauvages*) and holds that they cannot internally mature because they are at once granted recognition. We may characterize the situation by saying that the antiauthority ideology encourages these emerging pressure groups to put on their flag the demand for total power instead of compelling them to participate in the common good as limited associations.

If this is the overall strategy, what are the tactics of antiauthority ideologues with regard to the natural communities? The scare word by which its opponents label authority is *coercion.* We have recognized in authority (a) a rational reminder of man's social nature, (b) an eminently civilizing factor, and (c) a guide to the common good. The enemies of authority simplify and distort it by stressing solely its coercive aspect, and taking it for granted that coercion itself is evil. In this they easily succeed because pure coercion, which evokes images of torture and repression, is naturally repulsive to all thinking men, at least in cases when coercion is not a means of preventing a greater evil than coercion itself. Thus, it can be debated that coercing a man who has just placed a time bomb in a public place (movie theatre, supermarket, school, railroad station, airplane) to tell where the bomb is located, might be regarded as entirely legitimate since many innocent lives can be saved if he reveals his secret. At any rate, we are not speaking here of pure coercion, but of the coercive element that authority must contain if it is to be credible. Even parental authority, lovingly used, has behind it the support of coercion, should the child not respond to the attitude expected of him.[6] Likewise, since existence is full of contingencies and unexpected turns, those under authority may not be at all times informed of new decisions in the interest of the community. If, in such a case, they do not respond loyally and trustingly to legitimate authority, a certain amount of coercion becomes unavoidable.

Now, following Rousseau, the enemies of authority argue that in the course of his education the child should never have to confront human authority, only the obstacles that physical, natural reality places in his way. If he makes an unreasonable demand, the right course to follow is not in prohibition or punishment but in waiting until the nature of things will thwart his wrong action and prove it to be harmful or impossible. In our estimation this is dangerous and immoral; dangerous, because it adopts the policy that if you once burn yourself, you will henceforth avoid getting near the fire. But while this object lesson may be the only way to teach a young cat, the child is reasonable enough to understand the motive behind the forbidding authority. And it is immoral, because it assumes that the user of and complier with authority, the human being, has no way of knowing the rational and the good, and no capacity of combining them in the act of prohibition and obedience. If we take, instead of the case of the child and the fire, the case of the child and an animal he decides to torment, how are we going to wait for "the lesson of the object" without sacrificing, first, the victim?

Coercion rests, writes Yves Simon, on the psychological fact that a good habit, even when generated by fear, makes virtue easier inasmuch as virtue becomes internalized through practice. "Liberals fail to recognize the pedagogical function of coercion, and limit its role to the protection against bad deeds."[7] In other words, as we noted in our discussion of authority in the courts, if one limits the law's and the judge's sentencing intention to the protection of society against the criminal, one fails to perform the complete act which would include bringing the criminal to virtue (repentance, self-improvement) and compelling him to make the act of restoration needed for the social equilibrium that we mean by the word "justice." Instead of an action in depth, the law performs then a mere mechanical action. We have seen, in Chapter One, that the same principle applies to child-rearing: it is not enough to protect oneself from a child who insists on playing football in the living room, one must coerce him, directly and at once, to stop it and never to do it again.

The first act of authority's enemy is to weaken it in the family. In fact, the brunt of the attack on authority is concentrated on the family, where the future adult and citizen is brought to the rational realization of a small replica of the common good, a model of the institutions which will be stages of all his subsequent acts of citizenship. Authority in the family has been called by scholars *substitutional,* insofar as the parent exercises authority only as long as the child does not reach adulthood. In this interpretation, the child is deficient in the elementary social attitudes—as he is also deficient in knowledge that the school will a little later teach him —and authority over him fills the void. We shall argue, however, that no important distinction exists between substitutional and what is called *essential* authority, since man is always deficient in many areas so that authority is always rightfully exercised over him. On the contrary, the enemies of authority point out, not even the child is deficient; if he is allowed to act freely, his best impulses will come forward.

What is meant here by "best impulses"? Obviously not the habits directed at a civilizational order, but the "natural," "unspoiled" impulses which ought to be allowed to shape an "ideal" civilization. Here is the nucleus of our disagreement with the opponents of authority. Our thesis is that the child is born into a civilization which, if it is a reasonably good one, allows its members not only to live their lives according to a wise admixture of authority and freedom, but also to secure a wide area for them to effect changes in the civilizational fabric according to their talents, inventiveness, and rational judgment. The opposite thesis is that every civilization—and its subsections, the institutions—is repressive, and that the child is born a victim of forces he can never control, now or in his adulthood. Man was born free, yet he is everywhere in chains, as Rousseau put it, labeling once and for all the antiauthority attitude. The only chance of changing this civilization into a utopia is to set the child—*above all* the child, the still malleable being—free, released of constraints. The children taken together, as not merely one generation in the chain of succeeding ones but indeed the first really free generation, will then create a new society, a new mankind, closer to nature because acting upon good, natural impulses.

The seemingly innocuous notion of a "progressive" education thus turns out to be more than just another child-rearing method, it is the theoretical-practical foundation of a new and perfect society, without hierarchy, institutions, and coercion. It is for example alleged that without interference by the parents (see Rousseau, supra) the child would not become competitive, prejudiced about race, selfish, insisting on private ownership, aggressive—features condemned by progressive educators and opponents of authority alike. The parent is seen by them as the agent of an already corrupt society who carries his selfishness, prejudices, and so on, into the home and the nursery. Earlier utopian writers wanted, in fact, to exclude from child-rearing not only the parents, but also the domestic servants and nurses who bring to their contact with the young the habits, superstitions, and prejudices of their unreconstructed mentality. (We remember that Rousseau's Émile was brought up in exclusive contact with his philosophically enlightened tutor, lest he be infected with the unforeseeable but on all accounts corrupting influences of the workaday world.)

In this view, the ideal situation would be to restrict the family to two mating partners and to the mother's role of care-provider during the initial period, after which the child would enter the communal (State) crèche and school. His further contacts with the parents would be infrequent and supervised, and at any rate, permitted only according to the minimal demands of nature. The child's real loyalty and love would be channeled towards the community—represented by the Beloved Ruler or Big Brother—which gives him his sustenance and fills his cultural needs. All utopian books insist on the substitution of the family by the State; one of them, Conde Pallen's *Crucible Island* (New York, 1919), describes a kind of catechism that children must memorize as soon as they are capable of reading. Part of the catechism runs like this:

Q.—By whom were you begotten?
A.—By the Sovereign State.
Q.—Why were you begotten?
A.—That I might know, love, and serve the Sovereign State always.
Q.—What is the Sovereign State?
A.—The Sovereign State is Humanity in composite and perfect being.
Q.—Why is the State supreme?
A.—The State is supreme because it is my Creator and Conserver in which I am and move and have my being and without which I am nothing.
Q.—What is the individual?
A.—The individual is only a part of the whole, and made for the whole, and finds his complete and perfect expression in the Sovereign State. Individuals are made for cooperation only, like feet, like hands, like eyelids, like the rows of the upper and lower teeth.

It is evident at this point that the suppression of parental authority does not stop at the phase of the child's alleged emancipation from the family; as all utopian and antiauthority writers insist, another agent is supposed to inherit the parent's function, and significantly, the new agent is not just anybody whom the child may choose—for example, an older, wiser person—but is, without exception, the State. The logic inherent in the situation is flawless, even if inhuman: since the attack on the family is only the first phase of the offensive which is destined to dissolve all the other autonomous bodies as well, there remain no institutions between family and State—at least until such time that, as in Aldous Huxley's *Brave New World,* the family, too, can be abolished and children manufactured by chemical means in laboratories. Meanwhile, in proportion as the family gives up its natural functions, the State usurps them.

The process needs careful scrutiny because it seems today increasingly accepted. It is claimed that the shift from family to State authority in the matter of bringing up children is promoted by no particular ideology, but rather by anonymous social forces. How many fathers and mothers admit in despair that "it is too late" to prevent their children's estrangement and that the latter act like autonomous beings, not even claiming adult rights, simply behaving on impulse and self-will—and this in cases where authority and love had been inseparable in the family, so that no parental rigidity and inattention can be blamed. It is clear that the State as such cannot be singled out and charged with brutal interference, except in totalitarian regimes. What has happened, then? Neither the family's nor the State's fault (we cannot overlook, of course, the State's guilt in at least yielding to the legislators' will when they pass antifamily laws, such as abortion), we may rather speak of the absence of cooperation of all the important links in the network of authorities, a noncooperation of such a magnitude that one might say that a *counterauthority* had arisen in places of junction where the continuity of authority was legitimately expected. The family cannot fulfill its role alone, only in cooperation with other authorities in a well-ordered society. To take one well-known instance, there is no question that the media are doing their best to open a world to the young which acquires over their minds and imagination an authority that is taken away from the family. It is an autonomous world in which things happen according to a value system which is contrary to what the parents try to inculcate. Success comes to the ruthless, popularity is achieved by freakish behavior, and the traditional attitudes are scoffed at.[8] The young are confused by the powerful new source of suggestive information and find it hard to live in two contradictory worlds at the same time. Contingent events often decide which of the two they will choose.

A similar process takes place in the school. It has been long argued by educationists that in contemporary society there is no need for schools to teach subject matters because the informational environment has become so permeated by culture and knowledge that it has assumed the function of an all-round education. We saw earlier that in California, to mention only one place, the school program now focuses on the kind of "courses" that the young used to learn from the environment (friends, parents, life itself), and leaves the subject matters to the "environment," by which, again, mostly the media are meant. This is a complete reversal of the traditional approach, in the belief that society can now be trusted with the education of youth, and that the school is a mere agent of a subordinate character. In short, the school trains in life-adjustment, the milieu does the teaching [9]

The obvious reaction of students to this desertion of the school from the ranks of citizen-molding authorities is that not only do they not learn anything in school, but they are convinced that there is nothing anywhere actually to learn. Television and the street teach them scraps of disconnected data, and in school they merely acquire, at the cost of much boredom, the piece of paper which is the key to the adult world of jobs. Incidentally, they also see that the job world is as detached from serious dedication as the world of learning, since the teachers strike ritually every year and the professors deal mostly with daily politics, no matter what the nominal content of their course is supposed to be. Under these circumstances, it would be a miracle if any educational authority could survive.

The fact that authority is condemned to break down unless it can rely on other authorities in their common network is conclusively shown when we observe the process under discussion in the Catholic church. What goes under the names of "dialogue with the world," "aggiornamento," "opening of the Vatican's windows to fresh winds," is the church's vast shift to join the world and become its adjunct. This is not the place to examine the phenomenon in detail; I undertook that task in another work.[10] Here we may only schematize this occurrence of a world-historical import. During the past decade and a half the church has set out to beat her breast as backward, authoritarian, and structure-bound, and to recognize the world's superiority in science, values, and social concern. This is the total denial of the church's essence, since the church was not destined to be "of this world"; her authority now is based on something that the church no longer claims, whereas the authority she does claim as a social agency, does not properly belong to her. She shares it with other social agencies, probably more efficient. The consequences follow in ways which were predictable: attacks on papal infallibility (by Hans Küng, among others) and on the church's divine foundation, as also on every one of the dogmatic, doctrinal, and moral teachings. In the course of the 1960s the review *Herder Correspondence,* certainly one of the most important organs of the "shift," and distributed worldwide in several languages by the emerging *counterauthority,* systematically set out to dissolve and subvert the church's authority (her *magisterium*) on all points. I cite here the titles of a few articles to illustrate the strategy aimed at a complete reorientation: "The Theology of Revolution" (August 1968), "Intercommunion at Breda" (February 1970), "The Relevance of the Institution" (July 1969), "Good-bye to the Confessional" (July 1969), "The Priest's Uncertain Role" (March 1969), "The Demand for Married Priests" (March 1969), "The Church in the Ghetto" (June 1968), "Are Seminaries Essential?" (May 1968), "Must Celibacy be Compulsory?" (March 1968), and so on. What cannot be reproduced here are the political articles, the bias and radical tone of which are consistently far leftist.

In matters of authority proper, the position of its church critics (including the editors of *Herder Correspondence*) is that the church never committed her members to an unquestioning obedience to any specific moral law, so that the Catholic's approach to any moral problem can and should be based on his particular judgment, particularly if the latter conforms to the judgment of modern, progressive thinkers. This would make the church a mere advisor in moral matters—such as abortion, euthanasia, suicide, contraception, sex, divorce, and so on. But as Bishop William J. Philbin (Belfast, Ireland) writes, those who accept the faith include in that acceptance an obligation of conscience to certain kinds of church teaching, even though their personal thinking might sometimes lead them to disagree.[11] Philbin's statement is in perfect conformity with our position in this book: authority articulates a common objective, which, however, breaks down when the members question it on every point that strikes their fancy. The emphasis on individual conscience denies the common good (in this case, represented by religious doctrine), as if the worshiper's acceptance of the faith did not include the renunciation of his own favorite doctrinal position. The worshiper *wants* authority; he does not wish to set up his own faith and doctrine and change them as fashion and individual insight at any one time dictate—unless he subscribes to the aggiornamento theory of first loyalty to the naturally changing beliefs of the world. No better illustration of this exists than the difficulty nowadays experienced by religious orders as well as secular priesthood: young candidates refuse to commit themselves permanently and argue that they owe it to their individual uniqueness to change their "commitment" (no longer "vocation"—to be *called*—but "commitment"—to go along with—a significant terminological shift) under the impact of a new experience. The parallel with the constantly changing school curriculum is striking, as also with the young boy and girl who suddenly place themselves under the authority of a commune, a gang, a new fad, repudiating their parents.[12]

Antiauthority attitudes concerning the judicial process follow the same pattern. Like family, school, and church, the court, too, suffers from a crisis of identity based, in this case, on the denial of the legitimacy of punishment. This attitude is not derived from a general softening of the mores or from the spreading of charity: our century is more ferocious and brutal than many others so reputed. It is derived from the easily pinpointed self-doubt of Western institutions, that is, from the crisis of authority. Hence punishment as an effective method is not denied at all: terror groups hold hostages and execute them as a punishment inflicted on "society," on a "political system," or for some distant cause entirely unrelated to the person of the hostage. Vast concentration camps are established to punish those who do not believe in the priorities of a certain regime; "punishing" bombardment is inflicted on the civilian population of the enemy country; and so on. Thus, it is not punishment that is disapproved of, but the orderly dealing with criminal elements, since the enemies of (judicial) authority hold that the "new man" may not be penalized according to the norms and standards of the "old society." For this and for other reasons, the new man is not responsible; the part of his being in which traditional morality locates his moral sense is dissolved. Warren Allmand, solicitor-general of Canada, regards all crimes as symptoms of sickness, whether the rape-killing of four children (by 27-year-old David Threinen, in Saskatoon) or the murder of a policeman (by René Vaillancourt), both in the year 1975.

There is a curious reasoning involved. If crime is sickness, then man is good, since evil deeds are by definition never committed by healthy people. Those we call criminals are, indeed, good (even though sick) men, perhaps even better than the rest, insofar as they are victims of a society which refuses to treat them in what would be the only suitable way, medically. This is Sartre's argument all over again: the criminal has no awareness of committing a "crime," he merely acts freely, following his impulses. It is society, bourgeois exploitative society, which insists on labeling his act a crime—instead of regarding the act, as a socialist society would, as a valid new norm. Sartre is a good reminder for us that the enemy of authority, once he manages to abolish it, will want to establish his own. While all ordinary criminals are "society's victims," Sartre makes his view clear that political criminals (again, only those who oppose Sartre's ultra-leftist ideas) must be dealt with harshly, in fact, they must be exterminated. We remember that this enemy of all "bourgeois" law and courts became a leading "judge" on Bertrand Russell's "tribunal" which tried only such crimes that were allegedly committed by the United States and its allies in Vietnam, in Chile, and so on. In his book *Reason and Violence* (*Critique de la Raison Dialectique*), he elaborates the concept of "mortal solicitude" which enjoins the holder of the politically correct line to rectify his adversary's thinking by killing him if necessary.[13]

These observations lead us directly to the consideration of antiauthority attitudes in the army. In fact, we find here the rejection of authority as sharply in focus as in the family. Proponents of utopias are primarily critics of these two institutions because they see in them—namely, in family cohesion and in patriotism—the two main, closely-knit centers of resistance to the homogenization of mankind and the continuation of history according to strictly drawn blueprint supervised by an elite possessing total power. The antiauthority propaganda concerning the army assumes that man is good, and would live in peace with his fellows if some unreconstructed men, manipulating the atavistically surviving instincts and interests did not launch wars to quench their own blood lust and aggressivity. It is relatively easy to thwart such a warmongering drive since the army is a chain of authority. The action may take two lines: one is the discredit cast on army personnel as persons with distorted minds through the beastliness of military life and through obedience to meritless superiors. In this country this line was played up at the time of the My-Lai investigation: Lieutenant Calley could be pointed out as an illustration of inhumanity. One nationally circulated intellectual magazine showed four figures on its cover: a bishop, a woman, an average man, and Calley himself, all having the latter's face. The message was clear: we are all becoming beasts like Calley as a result of living in a nation ruled by the military.

The second line is more effective, it challenges the military from inside by attempting to dislocate the chain of authority. It is suggested in newspapers, films, studies, polls, and interviews that officers abuse their power, something for which examples may always be found in no matter what sector of society. Then the notion is launched to reorganize the army's structure in such a way that every rank might participate in the chain of authority simply by exercising the right of criticism. In the United States this is now a trend, since the sequels to Vietnam point to the army as the locus of great evils. Irate parents of soldiers put pressure on Congressmen to investigate the behavior of officers who had allegedly mistreated their sons. In other countries, the lower ranks are encouraged to form groups (soviets?) inside the army, to take up popular political causes, and to create division (class struggle?) in the ranks, setting enlisted men against officers, and so forth.[14]

These examples will suffice to show the antiauthority pattern since its features do not substantially change from one case to another. In spite of this basic similarity of action by the enemies of authority, let us state that the great majority of them are neither conspirators nor even conscious workers for a weakened authority. They follow what they believe to be a salutary course of action.

It stands to reason that authority can be challenged at either end: at the source and at its object, in the person (or institution) of he who issues the act of authority or in the person who obeys it. We distinguish two acts; they are, naturally, only one: authority is a function in which two unequal agents are united in a rational and structured act. We have noted that it is false to speak of "authoritarian" and "submissive" attitudes because authority knows that it is limited by the nature of the common objective, and the complier is similarly aware of the good he pursues and which transcends his own self. In inequality a structure is manifest which corresponds to one of the deepest integrative and cooperative aspiration of the human being.

Yet, the enemy of authority does not see things in this light. In the first place, authority for him is not rational, it is the barely embellished mask of brutal aggressivity; obedience to authority is a shameful humiliation in which the complier loses his human dignity. This modern view explains the success of the fancy theories of which Hegel's "master and slave" relationship is the contemporary model, and which helped Marx to formulate his pseudo-historical overview of "history as a class struggle" between exploiting and exploited classes. The dialetics of master and slave consists, according to Hegel, in the gradual appropriation by the slave of his master's consciousness, until the slave will be a complete (autonomous) man, and the master will accept the egalitarian situation, which for him is a defeat. Thus the slave—and those who speak in his name—

combats authority relentlessly, *in concreto* against his master, *in abstracto* against institutions in general which, as he sees them, embody the authority principle. The end of the process will come only with the total emancipation from all authority.

In the second place, while the enemy of authority believes in the necessity of society in a loose sort of way, he will deny at every opportunity that man needs social reinforcements in order for that society to be distinguishable from a chance aggregate. In his view, human beings possess all the qualities of sociability by which they may form a rather informal brotherhood of mutually helpful individuals, where there will be no conflict between the one and the many, the members and the whole. Quite inconsistently, he will refer now to the animal model where cooperation is, however, secured by instincts, then to the right of the individual to do as he pleases. While this is inconsistent, the double reference explains why the enemy of authority scorns and rejects institutions which, as we have argued throughout, are for human societies roughly what instincts are for animal herds.

Authority's enemy conceives of the human being as both animal-like *and* suprasocial. If man remains in society, he ought to be enabled to give himself the law by which he will live—and it is then expected, somehow, that these many autonomies will even out and establish, if not a society, at least a truce. Not all enemies of authority are so optimistic. B. F. Skinner, who represents a large segment in the antiauthority camp, believes that conditions on earth have become such that neither our animality, nor our rationality, can be trusted any longer in the interest of orderly survival. It is now time, in his estimation, to try out his own methods on a world scale, the conditioning of human beings towards the adoption of right behavior. Thus, in yet another case, authority thrown out the window, climbs back through the door, its function taken over by the committee of Skinnerian psychologists which decides the right conduct, an easy matter since they have designed the circumstances (the environment). Traditionally conceived authority understands the nature of contingent events which require authority in order to serve in the many unforeseen cases due to man's freedom; Skinner's authority, functioning only when man's irritating freedom is removed, eliminates contingency by organizing a world wherein the mechanics of behavior are regulated with total precision and prevision. But one legitimately wonders if the reduction of human beings to robots is not an even greater humiliation than their alleged enslavement?

Notes

1. See my *Utopia, the Perennial Heresy* (New York: Sheed & Ward, 1967).
2. *Le Monde,* January 3, 1975.
3. *Obedience to Authority* (New York: Harper & Row, 1974).
4. It would be naive to imagine—and here is indeed the limit of the communist indoctrinator's ruse and efficiency—that human nature can be fooled by these basically primitive methods. Families are more tenacious even than totalitarian regimes, and children learn '"to pray" to the Great Leader as they learn simple tricks. Neither they nor adults are Pavlov's dogs "honestly" salivating to the appropriate stimulus. The commissars never elicit loyalty to their pseudo-authority, only the required response given in fear and hatred.
5. *Nature and Functions of Authority,* The Aquinas Lecture, 1940 (Milwaukee: Marquette University Press, 1948), p. 45.
6. This is why the latest (1975) Supreme Court decision concerning the right of teachers to spank children is so grotesque. The enemies of authority exaggerate, once again, the supposedly horrible abuse that may take place, while they conveniently ignore the daily abuses committed by pupils on their teachers which include obscenities and physical assault. Even without the Supreme Court's absurd and ludicrous immixture in such a trivial matter, it is obvious that authority over children ought to be supported by the ultimate threat of bodily coercion.
7. *Nature and Functions of Authority,* pp. 52, 53.
8. A particularly shocking example was when the President's wife, Betty Ford, displayed in an interview her tolerance of free love, dope, and abortion. She showed in this a total disregard of the functions of the highest office, binding on the President's wife as much as on her husband. This function is to strengthen, not weaken, respect for the country's institutions.
9. Here is also the source of the "scrapbook approach" to learning which has subverted the teaching of subject matter. If the "world" as it happens to come to us is our teacher, namely on the trivial level of the media, then the correct method of learning is indeed to gather material from any source, unverified and fragmentary, and present it in place of systematic study. At one of the prestige institutions of the East Coast, a well-known university, one of the freshmen philosophy courses is "From Man to Superman." The misguided parents are very proud of this potpourri of pseudo-knowledge their children are made to ingurgitate.
10. *Ecumenism or New Reformation?* (New York: Funk & Wagnalls, 1968).
11. *Does Conscience Decide?* (Dublin: CTS, 1969).
12. The last few years' exemplary case is that of Patricia Hearst.
13. The enemy of authority, we said, ends up by positing new authorities, which, however, are not rational, but usurpatory. In progressive schools, writes

Stephen Toulmin, where pupils use words like "cooperative," "undesirable" and "antisocial," these words acquire the rhetorical force and emotional associations commonly belonging to "good," "wrong," and "wicked." (*The Place of Reason in Ethics*, p. 136.) The point is, however, that these substitute words are not rational; they do not correspond to the moral judgment contained in the commonly used words.

14. A recent case, mild in comparison with many others but illustrative nevertheless, was when sailors of a departing submarine compelled the commander to accept the presence of a topless dancer on board the ship. When the Navy command sent a reprimand to the officer and indicated proceedings against him, eventually taking away his command, the latter announced he would turn to civil courts to seek redress. Now it is quite probable that the officer first opposed the presence of the topless performer, a clearly undignified thing. He then yielded to pressure, guessing he would not be backed by his superiors, who do not like to hear about "troubles." When they nevertheless acted in a manner *no longer foreseeable,* he became infuriated. Note the reversal of the correct flow of the chain of authority: the initiative is taken at the lower echelons, the higher ones merely react in characteristic disarray.

5.
The Restoration
of Authority

There is an increasing, although vague, sentiment in wide circles that the presently spreading generalized anarchy in society ought to be stopped by the restoration of authority in precisely those places and institutions that we discussed in Chapter Three. If the sentiment is vague, this is because the thrust of authority's enemies, the partisans of the "permissive society of autonomous men," is dominant in Western countries. Chapter Four attempted to clarify that the partisans of a permissive society are not merely antipuritans or antitotalitarians, that is, people with reasonable views on life, civilization, and politics; they are basically antirational people who fail to think through the requirements that man faces when he lives, as his nature commands him to do, in society. More generally, they fail to see things according to what Jacques Maritain calls the "natural law":

> By the very virtue of human nature there is an order or disposition which human reason can discover and according to which the human will must act in order to attune itself to the essential ends of the human being. The unwritten law or natural law is nothing more than that.[1]

It would be, therefore, naive to expect to convert the enemies of authority to a more reasonable conception, unless here and there their own personal experience persuades them of the rightness of regarding authority as part of the human condition and, on balance, a positive thing. Even when he becomes suddenly aware of the necessity of authority, such a person hardly concludes from this experience that authority represents an overall good; he may argue that there is a wide discrepancy between what he experienced, on the one hand, and the general rule, on the other, or that even if his own case would warrant a general strengthening of authority in society, such a measure or law ought to be temporary and abolished as soon as society (mankind) takes a new step in the direction of the autonomous man and the ideal state of affairs. Let us remember also that in the eyes of authority's enemy, the "good society" for which he relentlessly works is not at all the same as the "well-ordered society," it is, rather, the structureless and noninstitutional coexistence of people of of mild and fraternal disposition where no coercion is ever needed. How could one expect the restoration of authority when the intellectually dominant elements promote, wherever they see a chance, the permissive family, free love, progressive schools, defiance of courts, the dismantling of the army, and protest against the State?

One cannot, consequently, expect to bring the enemies of authority over to the opposite view for which they have a deep-seated ideological aversion. Persuasion, more of examples than of words, can only go so far; we must realize that we deal here with a system of thought which, however unrealistic and anti-rational, is held with a great deal of commitment and intensity. There may be another argument against the antiauthority view, although equally lacking in full persuasive power. We may argue, namely, that there is always authority present in society, more or less naked, more or less disguised. In the summer of 1975, for example, in the midst of popular euphoria in Portugal, the abolition of censorship was, among other things, celebrated. One of the triumphs of the new course was supposed to be the takeover by the workers of the socialist newspaper, *Republica,* for allegedly serving bourgeois interests and thus being hostile to the revolution. The first act of the revolutionary-military government was, however, to appoint a team of military censors to the paper who had their office on the premises where they daily performed their task of controlling that the articles were not "antipeople," that no "wrong" epithets were used, and that none of the "achievements of the revolution" were questioned. The various sympathizing newspapers in Western Europe reporting about it described the censors' activity as friendly, benevolent, more a discussion over coffee than the issuing of rigid orders. Such a presentation is, of course, colored by leftist ideological stance which excuses the exercise of authority when done by one kind of regime, but not when done by another kind. Then it is called "authoritarian" or worse.

What separates the two conceptions about authority is the idea each holds of human nature, of rationality, of the substance of the community, and whether the latter is a mere aggregate of individuals or has a personality of its own. The enemies of authority are found as much on the political right as on the political left. If we limit ourselves to the terminology familiar to America, we can say that libertarians on the one end of the spectrum and anarchists on the other share a number of common beliefs about the function of authority. On issues like the legalization of drugs, pornography, abortion, and so on their conclusions are identical, even though not their motives. The anarchists argue that man is essentially free, and if there is a government above him this is simply by usurpation, without real rights to authorize or to prohibit; the libertarian argues that if at any time there is sufficient demand on the market for a product, it ought to be made accessible by legal means, provided the availability of the product does not interfere with the freedom of other groups to reject it, not to use it, not to consume it. The first think that the nature of man requires no government with a vested authority, the second think it irrational to establish laws of a coercive character other than a strict and neutral minimum, for example traffic regulations.

All this shows that if we approach the problem of authority's restoration from a certain end, namely, by encouraging individuals to act in the spirit of rational authority, to exercise authority in their own sphere of action—family, church, school, court, workshop, and so on—we achieve at best sporadic results, and at the price of great but isolated effort. Think, for example, of the recently very popular film *Death Wish,* where the horrors of civic disorder finally awaken a man of liberal dispositions to the realization that he must "take the law in his own hands." The movie audiences applaud him; but does he achieve anything substantial in the story? A few dead criminals. He does not stem the tide; his acts have a therapeutic effect on himself alone; society remains as disordered as before. He is finally advised by police to leave town. This inability of individuals to change public situations is important to understand, because it has become a ritual in our individualistic and liberal society for public officials, including presidents, to call upon the citizens to reject lawlessness, to be on the side of authority, of law and order. *If* people behaved in a certain way, they declare, *if* they became aware of the mounting disorder, *if* they made the resolution of reintroducing morality, authority, and respect for traditional values in the family, the public meeting places, and so forth—*then* society would improve its standards and regain its salubrious attitudes. Neither the declaiming officials, nor the listless society are aware of the tautology involved: the *if*'s and the *then*'s describe the same state of affairs, and the terms might as well be reversed: *If* we had salubrious attitudes, *then* law and order would prevail. In other words, all we have here is a futile rhetorical exercise which exposes our responsible officials' lack of insight into the deeper-than-surface substance of society. On the one hand, for example, they countenance, even encourage, the legalization of abortion—as when Governor Rockefeller vetoed the repeal of that law in New York State—then turn around and, with a notable inconsistency, deplore the disintegration of family life. Who cannot see that the legalization of abortion has a more complex effect than merely helping a relatively few women (the proverbial "hard-working, over-burdened women and their families") to remain this side of physical endurance? It opens the door to innumerable girls to lead a licentious sex life, to cause shame and moral misery to parents—and to further pressure for more radical legislation, forbidding, for example, husbands to interfere with their wives' intention to abort.[2]

Only when it is realized that the problem of authority cannot be approached from the "other end," so to speak, that one cannot leave it up to individuals and what amounts to their vote on the matter—may one begin to hope that its restoration is not a forever distant dream. One, perhaps the main, reason why the public officials content themselves with empty rhetoric but take no real steps, is their lack of insight—a lack of political culture—into the nature of *social being,* the interconnection of authority, freedom, justice, law, and morality. If, when dealing with authority which is a *public thing (res publica),* they insist on tackling it from the angle of the individual, they take the easy way out because in that direction the final arbiter is the ballot box. Some individuals, even the majority, may make a hard resolve to behave from then on in a certain way (like the hero of *Death Wish*); they remain nonetheless surrounded by resistance, opposition, incomprehension, and hostility. Chances are that the individual's resolve evaporates and that things fall back to their previous degree of permissiveness and chaos. We are speaking here of individuals who are not in a position of authority and who, according to the upward thrust of the subsidiarity principle, are the foundation of society, but who, according to the downward thrust of the same principle, need the support of the summit in order to fulfill their functions. Concretely, the public thing is not the sum total of individual things and cannot be remaindered to their multiple, dispersed, and intrinsically weak efforts. More concretely, authority exercised at various echelons can only be efficacious if it is *institutionalized* and is not a random thrust, disconnected from the principal stream traversing the life of a nation. This can be understood from the analogy with freedom: to hold that freedom means that everybody may do as he wishes leads directly to the permissive situation we here deplore; for freedom to have a sense—not in an imaginary situation such as a drug-induced fantasia can produce, but in a community—it must be embodied in institutions under whose protection

107

all can benefit by it. Otherwise, freedom is a slogan inducing a daily fright in those who do not indulge in the license that freedom encourages when its limits are not clearly and reasonably designed.

It is the same with authority: when sporadically and individually exercised, authority exhausts itself in vain because of unconnected efforts; restoration can only be effected from the "correct end," from the institutional side. But, it will be argued, institutions consist of human beings, they cannot produce more from their bosom than what their members possess in their minds and hearts. It is true that, taking matters to their limits, an institution engaged in a positive work but staffed and led by people with consistently lower standards than what the work requires, will in time cease functioning in the prescribed manner. A museum run by enemies of beauty and art would not long remain a place frequented by the public. Yet it cannot be denied that an institution, like the law itself, is not a mere aggregate of individual wills, efforts, and interests, entirely at the mercy of the whims of these individual members. An institution, like the law, has also an educative function, it is an embodiment (incorporation) of just such a function. We called it civilizational function in Chapter Two where we derived authority from the rational fact of men living in society—the Latin *civitas,* from which civil law and civilized behavior are derived, meaning the policed, well-ordered State. In this chapter we choose to call it educative function, because we wish to emphasize the roots of institutions in morality which accompanies the right education of man.

Human beings tend to regard realizations which transcend their own short lives and their own self-centered preoccupations with a certain amount of awe, whether these realizations are things concentrated by time, tradition, public respect, or general admiration. People pass by famous monuments at least with a fleeting reflection of what had gone into their conception, creation, and preservation. The busy tourists trooping up the Acropolis in the heat of an Athenian day to spend fifteen minutes contemplating the Parthenon pay tribute less to the artistic qualities of Pheidias and Ictinus, than to an object which has focused on itself the reverence of many generations. The matter is not dissimilar with institutions, although rarely do we concentrate our conscious attention on these invisible and intangible *collective persons* the way our senses are attracted by objects. Yet, even so, we are generally more willing to accept than to refuse the "message" that institutions convey to society; the overall reason is that we are conscious of their effort to improve us, to bring us a social-moral content in which a certain wisdom and competence have crystallized. In fact, we listen to (obey) institutions because of the moral-intellectual education we expect to receive. Such an education may also be derived from individuals we meet; this, however, is a random occasion as I pointed out when speaking, in Chapter One, of the charismatic teacher as opposed to the one lacking such gifts. Institutions are efforts to concentrate and render probable and systematic the citizen's education which otherwise comes to him or not, as luck dictates.

The public officials' encouragement that we act in the preservation of authority is irresponsible rhetoric unless these officials make sure that their words receive the compact support of strong institutions; these institutions perpetuate and, thus, render respectable (authoritative) the officials' exhortations to which society is willing to listen. Without such institutions the words and acts of officials (magistrates) are not mediated to society with sufficient clarity and persuasion. The situation is, then, one of *anarchy* as we see it around us today, or *despotism* when the officials use naked power, scorning the mediation role of institutions. At any rate, the absence of institutional guideposts and protective devices turns the public official either into an irrelevant and grotesque puppet behind whom the citizens perceive no conviction and no will, or into a tyrant who relies on sheer force to carry out his decrees, but who does not add an ounce to the status of authority in the community.

It is then evident that behind authority there must be the right moral perception *and* the political will to translate it into solid institutions. As an illustration of the first requirement, let us quote a conversation which took place recently between a group of California citizens, spokesmen for the Right to Life Society, and Senator John V. Tunney. The issue was whether the Senator would support a right-to-life amendment to the Constitution; the deeper issue, however, was whether he as a legislator understood the nature of law in general:

Q.—Am I right, Senator: You would not steal?

T.—No, I would not.

Q.—But it is all right if I do?

T.—No, if there is a law against it.

Q.—But why should there be a law against it? It is my personal opinion that if there is more money in the other man's pocket than in mine, I can take at least his surplus.

T.—Is there a law against it?

Q.—There is at the moment but we could repeal it.

T.—If you repeal the law then it would not be a crime.

Q.—But would you be against it?

T.—I think I would certainly be against it. I don't like thievery, but if there were no law against it it would not be a crime.

Q.—Would you try to pass one?

T.—If there were no law against thievery?

Q.—Yes.

T.—I think I probably would, yes.

Q.—Well, there you are, pointing out to us an instance of your legislating your personal attitude.

T.—But if the great majority of people in my state thought that thievery was perfectly all right, I am not sure that I would support such a law.[3]

If we are in favor of majority rule, it is clearly because we hope that the majority is morally right, or, this not being the case, it would allow the minority the chance of redress, meanwhile not compelling this minority to act against its conscience. From Senator Tunney's words an ugly specter stares at us: majorities could, after all, be immoral, and this immorality may go so far as to suppress the right of the minority to hold different views. Indeed, Senator Tunney could say this one day: If the majority of the people in my state thought that the suppression of the rights of the minority was perfectly all right, I am not sure that I would support a contrary law.

From what source does our indignation stem when we envisage such possibilities: suppression of minority rights or legalizing abortion? It stems from the conviction, articulated or not, that laws and institutions have a higher law behind them, one which satisfies the moral intelligence. This is why we want them to possess authority, whereas we feel horrified at the prospect of immoral laws and institutions being endowed with authority. At the very least, we wish to be reassured that even if the positive law and the newly created institution do not immediately join the moral law, the latter's validity is not definitively impaired in our community so that the situation may be regarded as temporary. The central evil of totalitarian regimes is precisely that the immoral law and institution are regarded as final (prescribed by history), and that the citizen is daily assaulted by usurped authority, without the hope of change.[4] What better proof is needed for the thesis that people need rational authority, that they expect to live in a society accordingly structured, and that they react adversely to authority's weakness or misuse? Authority is only mocked and despised when it is obviously antirational or when it is declining, when the men in power are themselves no longer convinced of its beneficial presence. Then, as we said before, they abdicate and yield authority to men more determined than they are. It is the immemorial experience of mankind, expressed by philosophers of history in various ways but always really embroidering the same theme, that the decline of authority leads to the permissive society, which then ushers in the rule of brute force. Ultimately, the problem of authority is a political problem. In America today, the effectiveness of a presidential exhortation that individual citizens should restore authority in their midst is about the same as telling the citizens of Czechoslovakia not to be afraid of the Red Army. We might formulate the problem in form of a question: is there sufficient political wisdom and will in the governing class of our society to strengthen the nation's institutions?

110

One may hide behind a certain type of historicist answer: there is a rhythm in the life of societies, period B follows upon period A with a certain regularity, like the seasons. A collectivity may get tired of too much freedom as it gets tired of too severe an authority. So let us be patient, authority will soon be restored, with a kind of automatic necessity. But this view reduces human communities to the level of biological aggregates; it implies, following the hypothesis of evolution, that there are tired societies as there are useless organs in the body: they atrophy and yield to useful, better adapted societies. Human communities, as distinct from mere biological aggregates, may have their own laws, but we will never find out what they are exactly, since if experiments were to be performed on societies, they would first have to distort the key data, derived from human freedom. The experiments would then be performed on a corpse, supposedly to find the secret of the living. On the other hand, all historical experience shows that authority is the chief guarantee of rationality in society. Who wants society, wants authority.

While this ought to be self-evident, we may consider it as remarkable that modern political leaders do not really believe it, perhaps because their tenure in power is short and precarious, and not tied to the common good. At times the evidence is brought home with urgency, as when the Portuguese prime minister, Pinheiro de Azevedo, tersely declared: "The government cannot continue governing under the pressure of political groups whose interest it is that it should disappear" (September 30, 1975). Similar statements could be made by a growing number of other prime ministers and heads of state, as indeed by family fathers, teachers, professors, judges, employers, and priests. Most of them are paralyzed not only by the enemies of the authority they nominally still hold, but also by the dearth of political theories which justify authority's legitimate use. With the ingenious formula "institutionalized violence," invented in the 1960s, these theories were collectively discredited in the public eye, so that, paradoxically, only the case for brutal repression remains, over against the various anarchistic positions. Any reasoned theory of government, law, state, or society can be now labelled a "rationalization of the interests of the ruling class"—against which not a mere theory of revolt seeks to be validated, but revolt itself, and immediately in its most excessive form. This is an unbridgeable polarization, and it may not be resolved by other means than total repression or total revolt. Whether they wanted it this way or not, the enemies of authority thus managed to sharpen the issue and decisively widen the gap between legitimate authority and what remains feasible under contemporary circumstances. How can one, for instance, still defend the essential, the moral, component of authority when an influential biologist like Julian Huxley puts on paper the following enormity: "Once we realize that the primitive super ego [the jargon

111

word for moral judgment] is merely a makeshift developmental mechanism, no more intended to be the permanent central support of our morality than is our embryonic notochord intended to be the permanent central support of our bodily frame, we shall not take its dictates too seriously."[5]

From the aforesaid, we may gather that no prescription or formula is apt to induce political, ecclesiastic, academic, or military leaders to restore authority in their respective spheres when that authority was allowed to collapse. All we can do is to try to establish the *conditions* of such a restoration, and in such an enterprise the historico-political examples will help us considerably. For let us bear in mind that *authority can only be argued for from a position of authority,* whereas anarchy is easily supported from the depth of anarchy as well as from the pedestal of power. Restoration, like all constructive effort, is twice as difficult as the spreading of anarchy, that is, destruction.

The question is then the following: what did leaders do in past situations similar to ours? They may not have had the same type of opponents to contend with as in our own time, but the ideology against authority is as old as the exercise of authority, and it always had ardent partisans. There have always been people like Dr. Ronald Fletcher, who writes: "Never accept authority; whether that of a jealous god, priest, prime minister, president, dictator, unless in your own seriously considered view, there are good grounds for it. . . . Rationalists in the modern world reject the authoritarian heritage of Moses and substitute a set of non-commandments, i.e., principles on which the individual must work out his own conduct when faced by particular problems."[6] One wonders what *authority* issues (or doesn't issue?) the non-commandments which tell individuals how they *must* work out their problems, and one is reassured again that the enemies of authority do not allow authority to fade away. If not Moses, then Dr. Ronald Fletcher is in authority. But we shall examine the problem on a more serious level than the one he proposes.

The restoration of authority is inseparable from a certain loss of freedom. This is inevitable since the absence of authority accustoms people to all the freedom they want. The habit of unlimitedness is hard to give up; therefore, the mere emergence of authority is perceived by those who had been most vocal for limitless freedom as a drastic curtailment. But it is enough to think of the examples of Solon or Augustus to realize this immediately limiting character of reimposed authority. From their and other examples we may put together, if not a handbook, at least an analysis of reestablished authority in its initial phases.

The worst thing by definition that can happen to a community is to fall apart, to cease being a community. It implies the vanishing of security, the loosened ties to basic values and to each other, the disjoining of the network of normalcy in thought and action, the brutal disruption of the process of habit formation. There are horrifying stories of the police strike in San Francisco (summer 1975) when police officers went on the rampage, beat up people with their sticks, and defecated in private cars after yanking out their passengers. The stories are similar of the firemen's strike in Kansas City (same date) where firemen threw burning torches into burning houses. Security is thus a question of political will, and an insecure society instinctively knows when this political will is absent. Its absence is translated into outbreaks like the two just mentioned, and also as the emergence of a myriad of savage power centers, each compelling the citizen to become *its* subject, each threatening him with a complete reversal of accepted values, hence of accepted conduct. This phenomenon can be described as a kind of *feudalization* of national life. It differs from the legitimate life of society and State insofar as the institutions run wild and the increasingly savage pressure groups compete, all of them, for unreasonable increase of their powers, finally for the supreme political power itself. What the thinkers on politics and the law throughout the centuries meant by a well-ordered society is a situation in which the *social orders* observe their hierarchical place and their general subordination to the common good. In such a situation, institutions do not attempt to expand their functions into areas not properly their own, i.e., universities do not interfere with politics, the State does not dictate family life, business corporations do not bear influence on school curriculum, unions do not break public order through so-called "industrial actions" (Great Britain) and politically-motivated strikes (Italy, France).[7] In their turn, the citizens possess, in such situations, a kind of reliable compass helping them find their way in the social traffic and identify correctly the institutional functions. Parents, for instance, who are concerned with their children's school work, do not have to accumulate new worries by thinking also of the political battles raging in the school which threaten their sons and daughters bodily and morally. All in all, our age, with its institutional undiscipline and social chaos, may particularly appreciate the fundamental plea of a political document like Plato's *Republic* in which "justice" means primarily that every institution performs the task for which it was devised, and no other.

But there is more to "feudalization" than what is obvious from the angle of the citizen's private life and security in their immediate scope. When the political will is enfeebled, a permanent power struggle takes place on the top levels of the commonwealth. The name of the antagonists varies from one epoch to another. In the Middle Ages they were the emperor, the pope, the lords, the burghers, and the parliaments (particularly in England); today they are the government with its bureaucracy, the political parties, the giant corporations and giant unions, the media, the pressure groups. In well-ordered societies all of them are institutions (so were "business" and "labor" in the medieval and post-medieval guilds), that is, single-function bodies. Let us imagine them as parts of speech, a not at all far-fetched analogy: every word is equal when taken in itself, abstractly, yet each has a different role in the sentence, e.g., subject, predicate, direct object, indirect object, prepositional phrase, and so on. What is clarity in sentence structure is order in society. Now in a "neo-feudal" society each institution, for lack of a controlling authority, is determined to conquer as much space for itself as possible, soon at the expense of other institutions, of the governing authority, then of the citizens. Marx spoke of class struggle, we may prefer the expression "war of institutions" as more adequately identifying the evil from which we suffer. Some illustrations of the mutual interference of institutions and pressure groups were given above; however, it is not perhaps correct to speak of "mutual," since, after all, it soon becomes a one-way process, the powerful ones dictating to the weak. The institutions which have become feudalities strive then for supreme domination, or at least for a share in the kind of *politburo* which runs things from the top. The second half of this century has seen the flowering of this type of institutional confusion each time that political authority was weak. Just as in the Middle Ages the lords, the church, and the private armies made attempts, often successful, to emerge as supreme civil power, so now in some countries the army, in others, the unions, in yet others, the party or the media grapple in the supreme power contest. With some simplification one may say that three main patterns seem to emerge: in the communist world the *party* conquers the supreme power; in the Third World, the *army*; in Western countries the outcome is unclear, for the time being the struggle for power seems to be resolved in favor of a central bureaucracy in symbiosis with co-opted bureaucrats from business, labor unions, and the media.

In this manner, we in the Western world legitimately call our state of affairs anarchic; future historians might well categorize these times together with those that took place after the death of Alexander or the assassination of Julius Caesar. The significant thing is, however, that by and large, people do not perceive this anarchy as a loss not only of security, but of freedom, too. A kind of healing power of the gods (or is it the veil of blindness with which they afflict us?) makes it possible for every society and generation to believe obstinately that it is the freest in history. True, it becomes aware of the spreading confusion and it makes a long list of horrors of which its members concretely suffer; yet, on balance, no society believes the whole evidence that it recognizes in detail, and more often than not, it rejects the risks of change from the pedestal of its self-hypnotized happiness.

The consequence is that societies suffering from anarchy make no serious attempts to compel their leaders to exercise the authority vested in them. To speak of American society, it is rather obvious that these leaders as well as other opinion-makers—possibly people at large—still believe in the self-rectifying power of the social mechanisms: elections, arbitration, law-enforcement through the courts, checks and balances, the plurality of the political process, and so on. They forget that "the order of human affairs is made in the making of history, and that if it is to be what it ought to be, it must be continuously created by ceaseless effort of reason and will."[8]

In the situation sketched above, it is evident that the political will resides less in the nominal leaders entrusted with the common good than in the representatives of pressure groups, whom we may refer to as "feudal barons," reminiscent of last century's robber barons. In the spirit of the American heritage, we may think of these new barons (whose visible concern is not to amass a private fortune) as legitimate spokesmen of pressure groups who, in their way, do the business of the nation. They are heads of powerful agencies, private or semiprivate interests, voluntary associations, but their weight is often enormous—not because of the wealth behind them, but because they occupy key positions in the new power structure of society, the bureaucratic-intellectual power structure. Americans like to speak of an overgrown government and contrast it with one of more modest proportions; but they forget that not only the State, pressure groups, too, can grow far beyond the optimal size. The growth of private organizations inevitably leads to the growth of public agencies, then of feudalities. Instead of approaching a decentralized State, we seem to be driving towards a monolithic one in which an ever vaster power is shared by a few monstrous feudalities living in symbiosis and weighing always more heavily on society—yet without relieving it of the evils of a chronic anarchy.

The restoration of authority seems to be, then, a much more difficult enterprise than it is generally realized. Political will that is lost is not usually regained by those who had let it slip out of their hands, and in the struggle for it one cannot unmistakably predict the winner. All around us in the world the battle is on for the creation of strongly centralized governments and the parallel suppression of rival powers. In spite of our tendency to dismiss the rest of the world as irrelevant to our own realities, we ought to stop and reflect upon the events in the Third World as well as in countries nearer to us with regard to history and institutional arrangements. In all Third World countries the decolonizing Western powers had left a democratic, liberal, pluralist machinery, the so-called Westminster model, as a heritage to the new regimes. After fifteen or twenty years of independence only, hardly any traces remain of this heritage.

115

India managed to last longest as a democratic, pluralist country: twenty-eight years after independence, prime minister Indira Gandhi declared that she cannot govern in a state of anarchy and proceeded to abolish the rights of citizens—rights which were anyway unused and unusable by the immense majority. In the more recently decolonized Africa power has not yet been handed over legally by any government to the opposition, changes take place exclusively through coups d'état, uprisings, and the massacre of the leaders.

Much nearer to us is the example of Great Britain. Reliable political observers note the virtual collapse, more precisely, growing irrelevance and paralysis, of the parties the efforts of which are checkmated by the threat of so-called "industrial action," the blackmail of suspending work on the docks, the mines, the metal industry, postal services, and so on. Lord Shawcross, with unimpeachable left-liberal credentials (Prosecutor in the postwar trials at Nuremberg, minister in the 1945 Labor government), writes now that Parliament has lost its traditional power and prestige largely because its members have become agents for enormously powerful pressure groups, the most important of which, he says, are the trade unions. The immediate consequence is the disaffection of vast numbers of voters, so that the votes of less than one third (twenty-nine percent at the last elections) "are forcing upon an unwilling people policies of which the mass of them disapprove." The alternative, according to Lord Shawcross, would be a government "patriotic in a true sense"; but the reforms he outlines he admits himself will not take place and the "suicide course" will continue. Let us add our own comment: people have been so conditioned by the network of ruling bureaucracies that they believe that the dismantling of feudalities—of this very network—would be a civic loss, the loss of the people's own freedom.

In a sense, it might be that. Because the reinforcement of institutions is usually itself preceded by a reaffirmation of the political will by a leader whose initial acts are, if not brutal, at least decisive. Since the tragic collapse, one after the other, of stable regimes during the period 1789–1918, the Western world witnessed such restorative attempts, from Napoleon to Francisco Franco; nations which were spared the turmoil during that same period have now also entered upon turbulent times the outcome of which is not yet clear. The pattern followed by other Western nations may or may not be repeated by them.

What happens to authority in such cases? We find it concentrated in one hand, the rest of the body politic being paralyzed both from the preceding process of decay and from the shock of its own sudden irrelevance. One may wonder at such times what sacrifices will be demanded for the restoration of authority in its first stages. Uusually, it is coercion. Will then the restorer at once proceed to establish legitimate and legal pro-

116

cesses, or will he seek to insert his own legitimacy and legality into the prostrate body of the commonwealth? In other words, will it be a new authority? But if so, it may not signify order and security for everyone, only for a segment of the nation, the majority but not the minority, or at least not immediately. From Augustus to the present this has been the scenario—unless it was worse, civil war. But it is hard to expect anything better; it would be belief in a fairy tale to imagine that on the first waving of a benevolent wand, order, happiness, and social peace will rule. A price is always paid when a people allows authority to be undermined, even if it does so in the name of justice, because justice too often means only the overthrow of authority. If our analysis has been accurate on these pages, then we grasp the fact that allowing authority to go by default, the community itself is allowed to disintegrate; the price of reconstruction is then paid in the coin of individual freedom because the first concern must be the *res publica.*

An increasing number of political writers, in the Anglo-Saxon world, too, subscribes to this analysis. They may not be willing to draw conclusions, but the premises are all there in their works. And in the entire Western world, as well as in other large areas, one of the questions insistently asked is what shape will the "new authority" take, "Augustan" or despotic? The longer we ignore the question, the more surely will the second line of the alternative impose itself.

The fact that authority is essentially *political* in nature does not mean that the individual citizen may retire from its exercise and wait until it is restored at the top. Efforts must be made at all times to restore it where it is weak or missing.

What do we find, indeed, in concrete circumstances? Probably, it was the experience of many people during the period of 1967–1972 to find themselves in quasi-revolutionary situations in schools, universities, and many other public places. The usual scenario was the violent interruption of peaceful gatherings or procedures by a band of "rebels," an attempted or actual takeover, disruption, threats, bodily and verbal violence, obscenity, and so on. Such occurrences were not limited to the United States; they spread elsewhere, too, like wildfire, to Western Europe, Japan, South America, everywhere except in the communist-ruled countries. In every case, one could distinguish several regularly recurring, moments, the natural rhythm and tactics of rebellion: the group which defies existing authority *becomes* a group only after the first success. Then it at once solidifies, building on the just-gained confidence. The successive steps depend on the quick thinking of the leader, rather than on the previously worked out program of action. But the first step, the face-to-face between authority and rebellion, is decisive, for a very obvious reason: there are two groups, the one represented by legal authority possesses the built-in strength of habit and orderly existence; the second group is not really a cohesive group until after it has tested itself in a confrontation. It needs the confrontation in order to exist. *If* at this decisive moment authority asserts itself unambiguously, the rebellious group evaporates; since some of its more hesitant, unsure members accept then to rejoin the self-assertive, legitimate group, the rebellious group may never reassemble again. The process is a psychological one; it takes place in the weaker, hesitant elements of the rebellious group; no such process occurs in extremely fanatical groups which have been lately operating, nor with groups led by exceptionally strong personalities. The trouble is, the history of the rebellious groups that have vanished in face of firmness cannot be written, because they made no history. Two successful group actions stand out, on the other hand, in modern annals: that of the Third Estate in June 1789, which was to disperse if Mirabeau had not cemented it together in a flash of courage facing the retreating royal power; and that of Lenin, who sent in a handful of soldiers to the National Assembly, ordering the members to get up and leave. Previously, he had declared at the Congress of Soviets in an apparent gesture of defying good sense: "It is not true that no party is willing at this moment to assume power. There is one party which is bent on doing so. I mean our party."

In the overwhelming majority of cases rebellions are not led by the Mirabeaus and by the Lenins, nor does the rebellious group consist of fanatics ready to die. Thus, authority has a built-in advantage. The experience of the late 1960s showed that the authority of the commonsensical view has a margin over the radical view, provided it makes itself clear, immediate, and forceful. The following scenario was current: a public gathering where all kinds of views were represented; a radical speaker who received the applause of a like-minded minority and who thus cornered and intimidated the majority; if in the right moment a firm and rational voice contradicted him, the whole atmosphere changed because the majority suddenly grasped the fact that its point of view recaptured the authority legitimately belonging to it but which had been left unexercised. Psychologists of the collective since Gustave Le Bon (as well as actors, public speakers, army officers) know that a group is a living organism, mostly amorphous so that the desired solidification can be effected by the correct use of authority. To this observation we add only the familiar but unexplored fact that authority belongs to the rational and the habitual. The challenging group must still engender an authority of its own. In most cases this process can be blocked.

What is said here about groups and ad hoc situations is true of established institutions as well. Authority can be asserted and restored over against its challengers in family, school, and elsewhere provided it is

118

systematically exercised and is not allowed to lapse. Provided, also, that one understands its nature and takes measures when symptoms indicate the coming collapse. Thus, years before the troubles in the universities, faculties debated at unnecessary length whether to relax the so-called dress regulations. They wished to be lenient at what seemed small expense, and finally abolished the regulations which had assured a decent appearance and a habitual feeling of respect for the institution of learning. The way we dress is habit-forming, our behavior is influenced by the kind of clothes we wear, orderly and clean or sloppy and dirty.[9] But it was pointed out in a previous chapter that authority's enemies do not understand the importance of habit formation, since for them the human being is a bundle of spontaneities. For this reason, university faculties were unable to see that with dress regulations abolished they had opened the door to behavioral excess and to contempt for school and learning also.

These considerations do not give us the final desired key to the restoration of authority. Enough has been said, however, to understand that the rational character of authority requires of those who exercise it—and, therefore, of those who restore it—the combination of rationality and will. A mere mechanical setting into motion of worn and lapsed habits, or, in the political area, of words and institutions devoid of meaning, must prove futile. Authority does not become irrational by the fact that *will* is one of its essential components, nor does it become tyrannical by the fact that it is an articulator and preserver of inequality. If a society, with its rich articulation, is reduced to an undifferentiated mass, it is not authority it will face, but the most oppressive despotism. Those who exercise authority must, therefore, have the courage and the will to lift—and keep—society above the temptations of the anthill.

Notes

1. Quoted in Leo R. Ward, "Maritain and the Tradition of Natural Law," *Modern Age,* Fall 1975.

2. In England bagsful of aborted fetuses are sold to cosmetics factories which use the fat in the manufacture of ointments and creams. There was a time when people were horrified upon hearing that the ashes of the cremated at Auschwitz were utilized for the manufacture of soap.

3. A Report on a Meeting with Senator John V. Tunney, Friday, June 13, 1975, Grand Hotel, Anaheim, California.

4. See the *Open Letter to Dr. Husak,* by Vaclav Havel, a Czech writer who illustrates with many examples the one overriding feeling of Czechs and Slovaks under the post-1968 regime: *fear.* Fear of criticizing the regime, of not repeating its slogans, of not denouncing their own friends, of not subscribing to more "volunteer" work, of not joining the State-sponsored groups, fear of having to spend their lives in frustration, regimentation, and submission. (*Encounter,* September 1975.)

5. Quoted by E. H. Erikson, "The Roots of Virtue," in J. H. Huxley (ed.) *The Humanist Frame* (New York: Harper, 1962).

6. Quoted in M. Jarrett-Kerr, *The Secular Promise* (London: SCM Press, 1964), p. 113.

7. This is not to say that students, as individual citizens, should not engage in political controversies and actions—but strictly outside the university and without dragging the latter into these controversies and actions, including the inhibition of the university's functions.

8. Maritain, *Freedom in the Modern World* (New York: Scribner's, 1936), p. 81.

9. A typical, and typically silly, counterargument at the time was that Einstein was nearly always sloppily dressed and would travel for weeks with a suitcase packed by his wife without opening it and putting on a fresh shirt. Geniuses like Einstein are rare, and they have the privilege of acting quaintly. Students and professors imitating his external appearance lack his capacities and are not entitled to the argument of "imitating" him; in the essentials they do not.

6.
The Nature of
the Restoration:
Augustan or Despotic?

Quite understandably, the main concern of this book is the possibility of authority's restoration and the inquiry into the kind of agency we may reasonably expect to perform it. At one point in the preceding chapter we asked, therefore, whether the restoration will be of the "Augustan" or of the despotic type. We shall examine these two only, because it has appeared necessary to dismiss the kind of restoration that the mental-comfort loving people like to envisage, namely a deus ex machina, a sudden happy functioning of all the traditional institutions, so that the citizens may say that the period of anarchy was but a bad dream. Fact is, decrepit institutions have little chance of being restored to health because their functioning is tied to acquired habits and socially approved values; institutional decline is a symptom of doubt in values and of interrupted habits. A return to them is doubly problematic: first, people lose their confidence in public realities which lack coercive power; second, the period of decline breeds and encourages new ambitions which, in contrast to existing but derelict public power, do not hesitate to use coercion as soon as the opportunity presents itself. In fact, they use various forms of coercion *before* the opportunity arises, hence they acquire authority—through show of power, promises, and terror—in advance of its legitimized use. Thus, in a number of west European countries, the communist party and

121

other leftist forces use a combination of terror *and* promises on their way to political power: on the one hand, they openly defy society and the State by creating unrest and anarchy on the streets, in the media, and institutions: courts, schools, factories, army; on the other hand, they engage in vast campaigns of reassuring the citizen that should they come to power, unrest, anarchy, and public insecurity would stop. It should be noted that in so acting, the communist party and the ultra-leftists behave as if no legitimate political power existed, and indeed the latter remains mostly passive, tacitly authorizing a kind of parallel government to address its citizens the way only a legitimate government may. Fact is, however, the citizens themselves lose the habit of loyalty and the respect for the law, and begin imperceptibly to obey the quasi-orders issued by the illegitimate, yet increasingly real, power. (Thus, in France and elsewhere the army conscripts begin responding to leftist propaganda aimed at the destruction of the "bourgeois army" and its replacement by a "workers' army" organized according to "soviets.")

It is then quite possible that the restoration may be performed only by the "right" or by the "left." We called the first "Augustan," so as to avoid allusions to contemporary controversies, and also in order to indicate the true nature of this type of restoration. Let us recall in a few words Augustus Caesar's achievement. Augustus was the beneficiary of the Caesarian heritage, itself not based on republican continuity, that is on the political tradition of Rome, but on a kind of "new deal" remotely reminiscent of our own in 1933. He also inherited nearly forty years' political and social upheavals in which the traditional classes (*optimates*) fought an intermittent civil war against the democratic forces (*populares*), a civil war in which the army played an increasingly crucial role. Before the young Octavius appeared on the scene, two conceptions had been locked in conflict. Cicero believed that the Republic could be restored if the old and new classes achieved a reconciliation: the senatorial class and the economically powerful "knights" (*equites*), those who through their business activities were increasingly important and demanded a corresponding political weight. In contrast, Julius Caesar was convinced that Rome would be reborn through the centralized, semi-Welfare State which grants the popular forces a suitable institutional expression in the person of a supreme magistrate with law-giving powers, a kind of dictator who may curb both the privileges of the senators and the uncontrolled activities of the business barons.[1]

The Augustan restoration combined these two programs, and, in the process of being carried out, they were permeated also with specific elements of the emperor's own ideology. It was, primarily, a military-backed restoration, as the term *imperator* suggests, meaning military commander. Augustus and the subsequent Caesars leaned on the power

122

of the legions, and their own power began to weaken only when the army itself became divided, each legion proposing its own candidate for the throne. But that is a later story. Backed by the army and by the popular forces, Augustus was able to perform the work of restoration—not only in favor of his natural supporters attached to his cause through Caesar's heritage, but also for Rome as a state and society. Finally, only the earlier backbone of the Republic, the senatorial class as such, suffered a loss of political power, even if no loss of economic power. Tradition, morality, and national discipline were recovered and preserved for two centuries, although the price may have appeared as high: the government power was now increasingly of a military character, and the head of State accumulated in his hands the legislative and executive power, plus the typically Roman power over public morality, which used to be that of the *censor*.

Our question is now whether this kind of restoration—the best modern term for it is "authoritarian"—is possible in our society today. Let us say at once that those who would be expected to initiate and to back it are not even necessarily aware of the "clear and present danger" of anarchy except as a rhetorical point to be made in public speeches and in private conversations. In other words, those called in America the "right" or "conservatives" are far from unanimous in their evaluation of whether the nation is threatened by disintegrative forces and ideas. The American genius for instant communication of news, ideas, and merchandise has a reassuring effect on the population which hardly ever suffers from want or from any feeling of being abandoned by the public eye. The vast migration to the suburbs caused by, and in turn causing, the deterioration of the cities as civilized centers, does not affect the political consciousness of the largely conservative suburban class, because its members feel protected, if not by what they see, hear, and read about the cities, which sink into anarchy, then by the fact that they do remain informed and up to date regarding even the bad news. In fact, they feel much more threatened by what the news media and the opinion-makers present to them as dangers than by the actual deteriorating conditions which surround their concrete existence. One should not be surprised by this paradox: people do not perceive dangers which do not immediately and violently affect them, whereas they do perceive such dangers which are presented to them with imagination and drama and through psychological manipulation. This seems to be the case with modern urbanites and suburbanites whose sensibilities are dulled because they are conditioned to believe that "*it* cannot happen here," the *it* covering such items as breakdown of order (that is, the smooth distribution of goods and services), revolution, civil war, external attack, misery, a liquidated civilization, and dismantled social structures. In contrast, this population is induced with an alarming ease into believing that "Watergate" was a national

123

tragedy, that the CIA and the FBI are covert instruments of a totalitarian takeover, that fascism was a serious threat during the Nixon administration, and so on. The power of the media over the American mind is such today that the imaginary danger translates itself as real through media insistence. The message which conveys it comes hourly in a compact form, creating a public hypnosis—whereas the concrete danger appears diffuse because it is underplayed, perceived as sporadic, and, most importantly, it is not presented to the citizenry by any source that this citizenry would regard as authoritative. Neither the media nor the politicians have any reason to point to the disintegrating structures with anything resembling the urgency with which they discuss Watergate and "repression."

The sources of real information are thus practically blocked, and the American people live under the guidance of an interlocking network of ideologized media. Lest the latter be taken only to be press, radio, and television, we should define the term as the "amplified voice of mass communication." So defined, we note that not only newspapers and television qualify as "media," but also, for example, the universities, which have become centers of mass education, and as such secure for their personnel, professors and students, a disproportionate and thoroughly ideologized voice in public affairs, a voice used in radical fashion. The population is consequently cornered by an all-round ideological presentation of all aspects of existence, including from sources generally estimated as objective, even scholarly and scientific. This situation has prompted Bruce Herschensohn to suggest setting up a separate government TV channel (or "time slot" on other channels) to give an alternative to the dominant networks.

> Government policies and points of view should be presented on one specified frequency or on a prescribed day and time on an hours-per-week basis on an already operating channel. By means of *sponsored* programming, this time slot or channel should be used for Presidential addresses, the President's press conferences, legislators' responses to his views, and by government spokesmen of agencies and departments.[2]

Herschensohn's commonsensical proposal shows a practical turn of mind—but it has little to do with the issue of authority's restoration. Aside from the great likelihood that the government itself would not accept it—precisely because it fears the media—and that the proposal itself would be at once attacked by the media as a shameless assault on freedom to criticize the government—a monopoly that the media take for granted—a government time slot or channel would sound barren in people's ears. In a very short time it would lose the little effectiveness it may possess at the outset, it would sound stilted and official, it would be timid, and it would lack the excitement that the media are able to generate precisely because of their critical, mordant, and radical tone. It must be understood—we discussed it at the end of Chapter Three—that the media are not merely an undisciplined, naughty branch of the information-enter-tainment complex with which one may establish reasonable arrange-ments, they are a *new political power center* with powerful allies and a loyally responding mass public, a product of the age of communications, but also of the age of utopia-inspired destruction of the State, of institu-tions, and of traditional morality. Herschensohn's suggestion deals me-chanically, in terms of the "fairness doctrine," with a nascent political power whose tenants are not interested in fitting into the existing state of mankind, but in creating a new mankind. They do not have to accept deals and compromises, they aspire at dictating the coming world order. They feel their own strength. Not only in the United States, but in several other countries, too, where Augustan-type restorers of order have been in actual power for decades, and where many sections of the media, like publishing and the universities, created their own power sphere in the shadow of, and tolerated by, the official power holders. Under the Salazar and the Franco regimes, in Greece, Argentina, Brazil, and South Africa, I could personally ascertain that the media pursued largely their own policies and presented leftist views undisturbed by the regime.

This is not the place to investigate the causes; I attempted to do so in another work, some seven years ago.[3] Suffice it to say that the "Au-gustan restoration" has very few partisans in America, and that even those few have anxious second thoughts minutes after the temptation has overtaken them. The very expression "Augustan" may frighten them since it conjures up the image of the military in politics, the censorship of literary works, a disciplining of ecclesiastic personnel and of members of the teaching profession, and, last but not least, a serious loss sustained by the political class (in Rome the senators, heirs to the assassins of Julius Caesar). All these categories have a vested interest in the anarchy they either created or allowed to develop, and, besides, they seriously believe to this day that either there is no anarchy or they are able to master it any time.

What are the chances of a "despotic" restoration of authority? The sentence contains more than one contradictory assumption: despots do not "restore," and what they create is not "authority." Yet, our century is witness that from chaos, rendered even more disorderly by the frenetic forces of the revolution, a kind of order was forged in which these same revolutionary forces imposed what one may call a "frozen state of civil war." In other words, they did not solve the social antagonisms, even less did they have a thought for the common good; they merely stopped the natural growth and activities and suppressed the healthy together with the anarchic elements, imposing on all the churchyard's peace.

The process, however, is not sudden, rather it is maturing through many channels long before the final outbursts, and nobody dare interfere with its growth, which is protected all along by an abusively lenient interpretation of existing laws and values. But there is more than this interpretation: the paralysis of both government and "silent majority." In his already mentioned book, Herschensohn speaks of sponsors of television programs which are in the long run detrimental to the sponsors' best interests, even if in the short run they help to sell products. And again he suggests that government should provide opportunities for program equilibrium, and so on. But what is the reason for leftist successes in the first place? Why is it that we face today the problem of leftist monopoly in the media? It is the very nature of what Auguste Comte called more than a century ago the "critical doctrine," and wrote that if such is embedded in the thinking of society, that society becomes impossible to govern. The critical doctrine is essentially and profoundly against authority, but it would be a mistake to think that its chief and most potent advocates are exclusively in editorial offices and among television commentators. They are also and more influentially in college departments, art and literary juries, and other similarly prestigious places. Television and press merely amplify the voices of professors, intellectuals, artists, and idea merchants and popularize their views. Thus again, when Herschensohn recommends, according to the old and obviously ineffective recipe, that the public write to the networks and to the advertisers (threatening the latter with buying the competitor's products), he misses the real target and evidences the kind of misperception that is symptomatic of conservatives and of silent majorities. For while people write letters to the manifest culprits, they disguise in their own eyes the real political and cultural manipulators. When a nation's major institutions—churches, universities, political parties, and tribunals—refuse their support to the value system on which that nation has rested, then the old methods of checks and balances, of warning signals from the citizens to the public officials, of extending the channels of communication, and so on, cannot be of much service.

To ask, as we did in the previous paragraph, whether the despotic restoration may be more successful than the Augustan one is a way of projecting the present into the future. But let us be more precise. The problem is not which one will prove more successful, but this: if the Augustan restoration fails, then the alternative is less a continuation of the status quo—since we do not have a status quo, we have a rapid degeneration—than the spread and victory of despotic ideology and method. While it is increasingly futile to expect an Augustan restoration, it must be admitted that the despotic ideology is ruling already in many areas and keeps extending its influence so as to form a network. The bare fact is that the Augustan reformers' efforts would, if attempted, run up against constitutional impediments, opposition in Congress and the courts, while a despotic transformation naturally ignores such obstacles. The Augustan reformers' reforms usually include the preservation of traditional institutions and methods, and one cannot expect such reformers to restore and abolish at the same time. This condemns them to a return, through a detour of exaggerated hopes, to their original position, which is to expect the automatic self-correction of institutions. Thus the following situation develops, well known from other historical instances: the legal-constitutional structure at one point begins acting as an impediment to the community's restoration and promoting, without intending to do so, the forces inimical to the community. Both ends of the political process, the operative laws of the land and the individual citizens, objectively help the cause of a despotic solution, the first by their rigid literalness which prevents the assimilation of revolutionary acts to common crime, and the second by their inability and ineffectiveness to organize and act in a sustained manner. The hierarchies of both public and private organizations, from the police department to business firms, cave in at the top, hierarchical superiors stop supporting the intermediate decision-makers down the line. The latter, finding no encouragement for enlisting the spirit and intent of the law in the concrete situations they encounter, begin acting, in order to protect themselves, according to the strict letter of the law—which is wholly inadequate in exceptional times. The laws were conceived and formulated for the average case of civil peace, and they presuppose an orderly milieu not substantially upset by ordinary criminal acts. Thus when the media attack public institutions and officials and promote a whole range of subversive culture, the positive law is powerless against them, and only an appeal to the intent of the law, contained in natural law (the right of the community to protect itself), may save society from chaos and disintegration. To pretend that the positive law alone exists, as our judicial tradition holds, is to tolerate aggression by armed men and to disarm the community's natural protectors.

Thus, with every passing day the leftist revolution entrenches itself a little more. It is in order to speak of a leftist revolution and no longer of liberalism, which was the language of the 1940s and 1950s. The ideals that, for example, the ADA defended in those decades under the liberal label are themselves attacked today by all sorts of leftists and ultra-leftists. The idol of liberals and of the Democratic Party twenty to twenty-five years ago was Adlai Stevenson; today it is George McGovern for whom forty percent of the American electorate was willing to cast their votes. At the same time, Harold Wilson in Great Britain is but an ephemeral barrier between an orderly society and the frenetic left-wingers of his own party, among whom not a few are Marxists; in France, Wilson's equivalent, the socialist François Mitterrand, works in partnership with the Communist Party; in Italy, in Portugal. . . . The conclusion is not hard to reach: a very serious shift has taken place in the last decade, with a decisive accelera-

127

tion occurring every year. The leftist revolution is no longer a mere verbal threat to conservative debaters, it is on the last leg of its march toward victory. In the late 1950s conservative journalist Ralph de Toledano could still write optimistically of "a radical-conservative reconstruction" and announce that times were "ripe for an American Disraeli." Unwittingly, he thus outlined an "Augustan restoration," although the man whom he was casting for the role was none other than Richard Nixon, a somewhat lesser figure than Octavius Caesar. At any rate, who would dare make such a prediction today? In 1947, another conservative, James Burnham, opined (in *The Struggle for the World*) that America was building an empire "capable of exercising decisive world control" as a victorious alternative to the communist world empire. Who could write such things today, thirty years later? Not even commencement speakers at West Point. Some fifteen years ago, conservative political theorist Willmoore Kendall elaborated his popular theory of "the two majorities," welcoming the solid *congressional* majority which regularly corrects and balances a more frivolous *presidential* majority. Are we sure today when Congress investigates and denounces our defense institutions and publishes the most secret intelligence plans that the power of Congress is of a healing and restorative character? That Congressmen are not as frivolous and irresponsible as Presidents and their advisers? Are we sure, with liberal-conservative Irving Kristol, that we are not drifting from a "representative, mediated government" toward a "plebiscitary democracy"? If, as it is foreseen by many conservative writers, the age of ADA-type liberalism has come to an end, are we sure that the post-liberal government will remain within the limits set down by the Constitution? That it will not be despotic in a leftist fashion and using leftist methods?

A look at the map will show that the number of democratic-liberal regimes is dwindling, those which remain are in a weak state, and the number of "despotisms" is rising. At many places such a despotism seems to be the only alternative—not because it is desired by a majority but because majority will has become virtually irrelevant in this post-liberal age which still runs under the liberal label. These majorities are now aptly called silent, and it seems they will remain so. The widespread belief is that the abdication of authority in the Western democratic-liberal countries is caused by the "bad conscience" of Western man: bad conscience vis-à-vis colored people, workers, students, Marxists, criminals. Such a thing would be hard to ascertain; it is probably a gratuitous diagnosis. It is more likely that the structure of the democratic-liberal nations has become worn and threadbare. It came into existence at a certain time (early nineteenth century) among certain given circumstances and for a definite purpose. The optimism which surrounded this birth took no account of the system's enemies; it was assumed that they can be educated out of their errors. The liberal-democratic system wanted to do good by all, its initiators and theoreticians did not imagine that their system, too, would produce marginal people, discontented strata, rational opponents. Entertaining utopian hopes about conquering mankind's future destiny once and for all, the system promoted its own desacralization (in order not to resemble any past system), it dismantled its institutions in the name of the mature individual who could take care of his own interests and knew what was best for him, it scorned patriotism, the nation's symbols, the need for authority. In brief, the liberal-democratic system allowed itself to turn into a nonsystem, a non-nation, a dis-society; its partisans believe to this day that the *res publica* is misnamed, because it ought to be a mere association of equals engaged in the pursuit of individual happiness, mostly economic. The indispensable minimum of commonalty is secured by an impersonal rule of law, mechanically applied as if society's members were parts of a machine. No wonder that when extraordinary problems arise, namely an internal aggression by disaffected strata, the system is unable, and unwilling, to defend itself. In the climate of positivistic relativism nobody accepts the obligation to tell the law of the community, which is the law of survival. As said before, the most commodious way out is to hide behind the positive laws—the consequence of which is a kind of solemnized drifting since positive law by its very nature has only one source: attunement to the temporary sociological picture. Once again, it is not bad conscience which drives Western societies toward anarchy, it is fear of the intellectual class which blackmails its opponents into submission to its own ideology.

Under these circumstances, it is hard to perceive the obstacles to a "despotic restoration." I am not saying it is inevitable, only that it is a distinct possibility. It does not have to take any of the violent forms experienced elsewhere; in fact the novel feature about the process in this country may well be its protracted character. The consumer society into which the earlier liberal society has degenerated following its own logic, namely that everything, ideas as well as goods, is merchandise, is able to slow down the coming of despotism, but it cannot combat it with equal weapons. The American people, like the people of other Western nations, has been so hypnotized by the communist danger that they do not notice that the revolution is plural and that it arrives with a whimper, not with a bang. Authority will not, of course, be restored, not even sheer order, only a kind of frozen state which permits the conformists to lead a quiet existence—hence its appeal—but it is merciless with free men. Its name may be "socialism," not the hypothetical sort which, we are told, wears a human face, but a faceless one which dissolves what remains of protective institutions, abolishes the political space in which the citizens used to move freely, and imposes a monolithic structure, a regimented existence.

Notes

1. Needless to say, the Greco-Roman political discourse did not contain concepts like democratic representation and "one man, one vote."
2. *The Gods·of Antenna* (New Rochelle, N.Y.: Arlington House, 1976), p. 138.
3. *The Counter-Revolution* (New York: Funk & Wagnalls, 1969).

7.

The Limits of Authority

We first dealt in this book with authority as it is exercised at lower levels of the social edifice, then saw its culmination at the level of political authority. There is no question that authority, from beginning to end, is a political concept, since it expresses the principle on which any community of human beings rests. Indeed, there are no alternatives to authority, it is the eminently moderate, because rational, principle for the preservation of order and freedom. It is the only principle whose exercise permits envisaging human beings not only as reasonably free *in* community, but also as legally reserving a large part of their personality for activities which do not fall under authority's purview. Thus it is no paradox to state that authority provides for its own limits; it includes the limits beyond which it is not to extend its exercise. Stated differently, authority is the guarantee that man is not totally subordinated to authority; the source of this guarantee is itself beyond authority, it is the divine stamp on man's soul.

From the fourth chapter on, we introduced another main theme, namely that the enemies of authority do not so much object to coercion as to the source of coercion when it is exercised in the name of authority. It was found that the reason for the discrimination is the will to create a new society, a utopia of autonomous men; but if among the "autonomous men" some turn out to be nonconformist and demand the right of realizing their autonomy outside of utopia, the enemies of authority will go to any length—far beyond what rational authority would countenance—to impose by coercive means their own utopian objectives on the recalcitrant individuals. We have witnessed this procedure in the last half a century during which societies have come into existence, from empires to communes, in the name of authority's negation, only to repress mercilessly the rebels in the name of an authority far more ruthless than any "authoritarian personality" could have devised.[1]

The opposite of authority is then an artificial principle which, although it, too, prescribes rules of behavior, prescribes them from inside a "new society," a nonrational society, one that human beings would never establish by and for themselves, one in which none of man's natural aspirations would ever be satisfied. Hence, coercion is ceaseless there, and its eventual success could be ascertained by the fact that the citizens are finally reconditioned to the status of robots. This is in contrast with authority the rationality of which is ascertained by the fact that it does not have to be used all the time, since its directives coincide with what rational men regard as rational, thus valid and natural to follow. This rationality would be further ascertained by the vastness of the area on which authority claims no right of trespass.

In the following, we shall attempt to examine the limits of authority, first by considering two artificial patterns of society which today are fashionable, then by considering the nature of these limits in view of the area lying beyond them.

There are today, in the so-called human sciences, two contending schools of thought about how to control mankind's future, which both judge as critical. One school of thought may be called *environmentalist*, the other *evolutionist*. The argument of the first may be summed up as follows: man's origin is animal, he is an offshoot of the primates. But in man's case, the animal instincts have consistently receded so that he is at the present stage more rational than animal, able and ready to control his environment in such a manner as to derive from it optimal conditions. Contrasted with other primates, what makes man human is the control of behavior he can exercise over his habitat, the whole earth. In America, this theory is represented by Franz Boaz and his disciples. As one of them, Margaret Mead, puts it, "Human culture depends neither on instincts, nor on habits transmitted through heredity, but on acquisitions slowly accumulated with the help of a continuous readjustment."[2] This view leads directly to the assumption that nothing is inherent in human nature—except a kind of endlessly empty ability to adjust—and, in the second place, that a suitably arranged environment would produce a very different, new man. Such men would not contain any trace of *evil* in their

132

character, since the environment would mold them in the view of *good* only. Another anthropologist, Ashley Montagu, writes this: "Evil is not inherent in human nature, it is learned. . . . Aggressivity is an acquisition, like all other forms of violence, too."[3] The man-molding experiments of B. F. Skinner are designed to prove the same point. According to the combined view, *evil* (in whichever way we wish to define it) could be eliminated from the environment, consequently from the storehouse where new character traits can be selected for the new man, and *good* could be redesigned also to mean what the experimenters wish to emphasize as positive. In this way, the experimenters would become more than a ruling elite, more than a caste; they would be literally gods creating an entirely new being by environment manipulation. The citizen, if the status still applies, would by no means be an "autonomous man," he would be a robot like the alpha, beta, gamma, and delta types whom a team of world controllers manipulates in Aldous Huxley's *Brave New World,* after having manufactured them in the laboratory. In such a world, there is no authority; it is replaced by the certainty of adjusting mechanical parts to other mechanical parts. Authority always has a precarious edge on account of the freedom of those over whom it is exercised, and also on account of the freedom of the person in authority to modify his own role. The value of the esprit de corps in an army unit is that both officers and soldiers obey orders not mechanically, but by an act of consent of mind and will. In the society managed by the environmentalist engineers the citizen's behavior is prefabricated and so is the interaction between him and his manipulator. If anything remains uncertain, it is the latter's behavior, unless he, too, is preprogrammed in such a way as to apply the same formula without fail at all times.

The evolutionist school's argument apparently opposes the environmentalist position, but it turns out to be its twin. Mankind's crisis, in the environmentalist view, consists of our still inadequate means of environment control, due in large measure to the survival of people who remain attached to the traditional concept of man's freedom, the imperfect societies in which man lives, even the risks he must take in order to find his imperfect happiness. The crisis, seen by the evolutionist, consists of man's lack of understanding of his biological heritage and its implications. Seventy million years, the anthropologist Lionel Tiger writes, have so programmed us that we are bent on reproducing ourselves limitlessly, because that is what our ancestors always did. Biosociology must now be allowed to take charge of our future, we must take a "veterinarian view of the species so as to prevent man from overpopulating himself to death."[4] Other anthropologists, like Konrad Lorenz, Robert Ardrey, Eibl-Eibesfeldt, and others, deplore other aspects of the crisis: the lessening of challenges facing youth, especially in the West, the overall condemnation of "aggression" when, in reality, man cannot live without some form of it: competition, rivalry, adventure, risk. In contrast to the environmentalists, the evolutionists insist on the presence of animal instincts in our makeup; they show through comparative studies the extent to which we have merely modified, but did not extirpate, the instinctual features from our behavior. The environmentalists argue that man is a product of society; the evolutionists retort that this is true only to a limited extent, more to the point is that man is the product of a long line of animals which determines his nervous system and his sensory organs. Aggressivity, therefore, is not something acquired (and capable of being eliminated), it is an innate instinct. The world that the evolutionists would like to see emerge from the present crisis would be one in which, as Robert Ardrey writes, a new "social contract" would be established: since a society of equals is impossible because of the unequal talents with which men are endowed, a *biopolitics of social selection* would constitute the main principle of public action. In his *Natural Law,* Ardrey elaborates on the subject: all superior primates from hierarchical groups, and efficiency is in direct proportion to the strictness of the hierarchy. The latter is then a biological requirement which does not prevent, but promotes, the "competition of unequals," illustrated by research on the rhesus monkey of India. We are not surprised at the characteristic words in which Ardrey describes the difference between Rousseau's and his own social contract: the participants of Rousseau's social contract are "fallen angels" (fallen from the state of natural equality, one assumes), the participants of Ardrey's are "evolved monkeys."

It seems that Mead, Montagu, Skinner, and so on, desire a society of *machines,* only then do they feel reassured that mankind, stumbling from crisis to crisis, will preserve itself, and more: perfect itself through the elimination of "bad" character traits in favor of "good" ones. The two terms are defined according to the anthropologist-social engineer's value system, arrived at in ways that the uninitiated knows nothing about. Whether a society of robots is worth preserving is, of course, a question that one cannot decide *within* the Skinnerian value system, only outside it, and then the Skinnerian system becomes one of the data of the judgment. Ardrey, Tiger, and so on, on the other hand, desire a society of *superior primates;* only then do they feel reassured that mankind, stumbling from one crisis to the next, will preserve itself through the elimination of the temptations of an unchallenging existence in favor of a hierarchical and competitive system. While we do not oppose challenge and competition, we might not wish to (a) conceive them merely in animal-instinctual terms, nor (b) submit ourselves to the biological control of "veterinarians" in order to secure the system against the temptations of softness. Again, whether a society of men treated as superior primates, a zoo with a laboratory annex, is worth preserving, can only be decided from outside the system which sets it up.

In both the environmentalist and evolutionist systems authority is eliminated because neither system resembles a human community. The cases they illustrate permit us to measure through their extremism the limits of authority. Authority as said above is not to be regarded as the lid on a hermetically closed and explosive situation, it is not a scientifically devised, mechanical guarantee against all conceivable possibilities. The repulsiveness of the two above described positions resides in the double fact that they regard the human situation as standing on the brink of imminent collapse and as corrigible only if drastic remedies, proposed by them, are adopted. On closer scrutiny we find, rather, that their particular view of man and society is such that from *its* perspective, mankind is indeed irremediably condemned to a horrible fate, and that salvation can only come if a different mankind is urgently constructed. Authority, on the other hand, is a concept derived from the state of mankind as it is by nature, an always "critical" state in the sense that it is forever a battlefield of freedom and coercion, of good and evil, of individual aspiration and communitarian objectives. A "battlefield," as just said, but the term implies no state of emergency, no urgent need for a "peaceful solution"; it only means creaturely imperfection, which, however, grants us enough lucidity to see what we ought to do in the moral order, even if it is often thwarted in the practical order. The "crisis view" of society (and of mankind) is apparently horrified at human imperfections and limitations, yet it fails to take into consideration that the remedies it proposes are also fraught with imperfections, first of all the limitations and temporary character of the very science in whose name the remedy is proposed. For suppose that the next day new light is shed on the mysteries of human behavior or of evolution; could one then undo the new society which had been "scientifically" reoriented by today's biosociological veterinarian or mechanistic social engineer?

One limitation on authority is, consequently, the "no trespass" line beyond which society would be so mechanically organized that the citizen robots have neither rationality nor free will to accept or reject the power over them. Everything we said in the first chapters about the nature of authority suggests that we meant its exercise exclusively within the framework of rationality and freedom of will. We agreed to some extent with the environmentalists that man has weak instincts and much rationality so that he needs social reinforcements—but we disagree emphatically when told that these reinforcements may remain rational when a behavioral conditioning makes them absolute and foolproof. We agree willingly with the evolutionists that there is a natural inequality among men and that society rests on it, but we regard authority as the agency which secures orderliness for this inequality—and we reject the view that inequality ought to be guaranteed by the same rigid hierarchy that exists among "evolved apes" and *because* we are such apes, too. What both schools of thought miss, whereas we emphasized it, is that authority is not *bad* (as the environmentalists say) or *good* (the evolutionist view), it points towards a good which is not only social, but also ethical in nature. Without authority not only ordinary social objectives cannot be achieved, the fullness of our human vocation cannot be approximated, either. We human beings are links in the social and political order, in view of social-political objectives; we are links in the transcendental order also, in view of a divinely appointed purpose, and in this sense we accept authority as an ordering principle leading to a better life: contemplation, charity, sacrifice.

Where would one locate authority's mediating function between a higher law and the individuals if the only existing landscape were that of the environmentalists and of the ethologists? There is no higher law for conditioned man, hence no authority, only power. Authority is inseparable from freedom, which in turn needs authority's restraint in order not to degenerate into forms of non-freedom: slavery, anarchy, rigidity. At this point we meet the inherent limit of authority. It was classically illustrated by Sophocles' play *Antigone* where the princess defies the State's law in the name of a higher law, piety. Sophocles, however, did not settle the question; it is debated anew in every country, generation, and circumstance. But only the degree of apportioning the primacy of the higher law is debated every time, not the fact that this law is indeed higher. The debate deviates from its course because it is implicitly assumed that authority is always only State authority, and that the conflict takes place, therefore, between the *raison d'état* and the individual's conscience. Then, according as the debaters adopt a "hard" or a "soft" position, their exchange continues endlessly: they neglect to discuss the nature of authority.

Animals are integrally members of their herd, human beings only partially since they possess rational motives for their membership, they discern the good and the bad involved. The rational motive, expressed by Cicero whom we quoted at the beginning, is that men are by their nature attracted to the company of other men so as to improve and enrich one another and seek higher achievements in commonalty, in arts, industry, and intellectual-spiritual endeavors. They enjoy this association within the orderly society, to be sure, but the condition of enjoyment is the freedom to make, to produce, to achieve, to create, to contemplate. The role of authority here is one between guardianship and benign neglect: it is in their freedom that individuals are able to do things which make

136

additions to the community and beyond it to what we may call the "cultural patrimony." A great symphony or a scientific discovery is not made for the community or under authority; yet the free act returns to the community and adds to its volume and stature, it is inseparable from it, it would not have come into existence without it.

It is rationality also which tells us that there are higher and lower planes than the fact of belonging to society—but only in the sense that on these planes we belong to a different kind of society. For instance, there are many aspects of personal life—love is one—which, in their essence, are outside the scope of social order, and there are many aspects of a higher dedication—religion is one—which also escape social scrutiny. This is why it may be said that man is both smaller and greater than society (or the State), and that, at any rate, he transcends the social (and political) limitations of authority. But to claim it legitimately, he must first satisfy the imperatives of his membership in society and the body politic. This requirement must be understood in the spirit of what Maritain means when he writes:

> The order of good moral and civil administration prescribes that publicans and prostitutes shall take rank after persons of honorable life. The order of the Kingdom of Heaven permits publicans and prostitutes to take rank, in the inscrutable judgment of God, before persons of honorable life.[5]

The human and the divine standards may overlap, but they are different: the first should be applied in the temporal community and always with an edge of doubt as to its essential rightness, yet firmly, because our wisdom cannot transcend our condition.[6]

But man's transcendence of society does not consist of wild, anarchic acts, it has to be interpreted *within* society's order, precisely where authority reaches its natural limit. The meaning of this is not that authority ought to be exercised with moderation and circumspection; this must is taken for granted by the fact that it aims at the common good. The point is that the individual is able by himself to go where authority leads him, and beyond it. We said earlier that authority has an educative function; this is true but one must make room also for the autodidact who reaches the good life through his own efforts. Political authority does not have rivals only; it also has fraternal allies.

Notes

1. Although the Roman State is usually regarded as the epitome of *raison d'état* and ruthless power, it would be interesting to draw a detailed comparison between how that State treated its citizens in civil and criminal cases (arrest, investigation, freedoms guaranteed while in detention) and how the Soviet State treats its citizens. Such a comparison might begin with the cases of St. Paul and Aleksandr Solzhenitsyn.

2. Margaret Mead and Ruth L. Bunzell (eds.), *The Golden Age of American Anthropology* (New York: Braziller, 1960).

3. *The Humanization of Man* (World Press, 1962).

4. From an interview with Dom Moraes, *Voices for Life: Reflections on the Human Condition* (New York: Praeger, 1975).

5. *Freedom in the Modern World*, p. 78.

6. This idea is magnificently expressed in a medieval legal text which recommends that a representation of the Last Judgment be placed in courtrooms because "wherever the judge sits in judgment, there, and in the same hour, God is sitting in his divine judgment above the judge and the jury." Otto von Simson, *The Gothic Cathedral* (New York: Pantheon, 1956), p. 182.

Index

ACLU. *See* American Civil Liberties Union
ADA. *See* Americans for Democratic Action
Adorno, Theodore, 81, 82, 83, 85
Alexander the Great, 114
Allmand, Warren, 98
Althusius, 68
Americans for Democratic Action (ADA), 127
Antiauthoritarians, 78–101; dehumanization by, 88–91; Frankfurt School, 82–84; Milgram experiment, 84–86
Antigone, 136
Ardrey, Robert, 19, 26, 133, 134
"Are Seminaries Essential?," 97
Aristotle, 23, 35
Augustus, 112, 117, 122–123, 128
Authoritarian Personality, The, 82, 85
Authoritarians and authoritarianism, 78
Authority: analogous to love, 9–10; in the army, 59–64, 99–100; "Augustan" restoration of, 122–125; bases of, 18–20; charismatic, 12–13,
18; in the church, 39–44, 96–98; and the courts, 44–49, 98–99; "despotic" restoration of, 125–129; in the family, 31–34, 93–96; functions of, 79; groups and, 11–12, 15–18, 117–118; the individual and, 10–11; and inequality, 23–25, 26, 79, 135–136; institutional, 12–14; in international relations, 70–74; limits of, 132–137; in literature and art, 54–59; need to be institutionalized, 106–111; philosophy of, 25–27; a political concept, 131; rationality of, 78–79, 110–111, 132; restoration of, 104–119, 121–129; in the school, 34–38, 94, 96; and the State, 64–70; in the workshop, 49–54
Azevedo, Pinheiro de, 111

Baader-Meinhof band, 90
Baudelaire, Charles, 56
Bloch, Marc, 39
Boaz, Franz, 132

139

Bodin, Jean, 68
Boyle, Captain Richard, 64
Brave New World, 95, 133
Brinton, Crane, 18
Burnham, James, 128

Caesar, Julius, 114, 122, 123, 125
Caesar, Octavius. *See* Augustus
Calley, Lieutenant William, 99
Campbell, Dr. Donald T., 86, 87
Carlsson, Minister of Education, 38
Censorship, 55–59, 105
Chaplin, Charlie, 78
"Childhood of a Leader" (*L'Enfance d'un Chef*), 88
Chomsky, Professor Noam, 59
"Church in the Ghetto, The," 97
Cicero, 15, 122, 136
Coercion, 92–93, 116–117, 121–122, 131–132
Columbia University, 82
Comte, Auguste, 126
Crucible Island, 95

Daniélou, Jean Cardinal, 7
De Corte, Marcel, 33, 45
De Republica, 15
de Toledano, Ralph, 128
Death Wish, 106, 107
"Demand for Married Priests, The," 97
Dewey, John, 7, 33, 36, 80
Dumézil, Georges, 59–60

Eibl-Eibesfeld, Irenaeus, 21, 133
Eliade, Mircea, 86, 87
Engels, Friedrich, 50
Environmentalists vs. evolutionists, 132–136
Erikson, Erik, 26, 81, 86
European Revolution, The, 71–72
Eysenck, H.J., 26–27

Feudalization, 113–115
Fletcher, Dr. Ronald, 112
Flowers of Evil, The, 56
Franco, Francisco, 116, 125

Frankfurt School 82–83, 85, 87, 88
Friedrich, Professor Carl J., 23, 43–44
Fromm, Erich, 81

Galileo, 56
Gandhi, Indira, 116
Gide, André, 57
Gierke, Otto, 66–67
Goodall, Jane, 19, 21
"Good-bye to the Confessional," 97
Goubert, Pierre, 55
Grotius, Hugo, 68
Guevara, Ché, 89
Gulag Archipelago, The, 49

Hegel, Georg W. F., 100
Herder Correspondence, 97
Herschensohn, Bruce, 124–125, 126
Hierarchy, 17–18, 113
Hitler, Adolf, 61
Hobbes, Thomas, 67, 68
Horkheimer, Max, 81, 82, 85, 89
Huntford, Robert, 38
Huxley, Aldous, 95, 133
Huxley, Julian, 111–112

"Inner-directed" man, 7–8
"Intercommunion at Breda," 97

Jaccard, Roland, 81
James I (England), 25
Janick and Toulmin, 58
Jefferson, Thomas, 66
Jesuit Secondary Education Association (JSEA), 38

Kendall, Willmoore, 128
Kierkegaard, Sören Aabye, 41–42, 43
Kolakowski, Leszek, 43
Kristol, Irving, 128
Küng, Hans, 97

Lamb, Ursula, 20
Le Bon, Gustave, 118
Le Figaro, 90

Lenin, Nikolai, 118
Locke, John, 66, 68
Lonely Crowd, The, 7
Lorenz, Konrad, 19, 26, 33, 133
Lowenthal, Professor Richard, 50–51

McGovern, George, 127
Maistre, Joseph de, 46
Manson family, 90
Mao Tse-tung, 89
Maritain, Jacques, 104, 137
Marx, Karl, 50, 52, 82, 100, 114
Mead, Margaret, 132, 134
Milgram, Professor Stanley, 80, 81, 84–
    86, 87, 89, 91
Mirabeau, 118
Mitterrand, François, 127
Montagu, Ashley, 133, 134
Montesquieu, 70–71
Moscardo, Colonel, 24
Moses, 112
Mussolini, Benito, 78
"Must Celibacy Be Compulsory?," 97

Napoleon, 116
Natural law, 104
Natural Law, 134
New Totalitarians, The, 38
Newman, John Henry Cardinal, 44
Nixon, Richard, 128

Obedience to Authority, 80, 81, 85
"Other-directed" man, 7

Pallen, Conde, 95
Pascal, Blaise, 41
Philbin, Bishop William J., 97–98
Plato, 60, 113
Polanyi, Karl, 53
"Priest's Uncertain Role, The," 97

*Reason and Violence (Critique de la
    Raison Dialectique),* 99
"Relevance of the Institution, The,"
    97
Republic, The, 113

Republica, 105
Ricoeur, Paul, 92
Riesman, David, 7
Right to Life Society, 109–110
Rockefeller, Governor Nelson A., 107
Rousseau, Jean Jacques, 10, 91, 92, 94,
    134
Russell, Bertrand, 99

St. Francis, 18
Saint Genet, Comedian and Martyr, 47
St. Ignatius, 18
St. Paul, 25
Salazar, Antonio de Oliveira, 125
Sartre, Jean-Paul, 47, 88, 99
Schorr, Helmut, 26
Schumpeter, Joseph, 50
Seitz, Bishop, 90–91
Shawcross, Lord, 116
Simon, Yves, 91, 93
Skinner, B. F., 26, 101, 133, 134
"Social rationality," 16–17
Socrates, 56
Solon, 112
Solzhenitsyn, Aleksandr, 49, 80
Sophocles, 136
Spock, Dr. Benjamin, 80
Stalin, Josef, 80
Stevenson , Adlai, 127
Storr, Anthony, 21
Strachey, John, 50, 51
Struggle for the World, The, 128
Sulzman, Father William, 64
Summerhill (school), 33–34

Tagesspiegel, 49
"Theology of Revolution, The," 97
Tiger, Lionel, 133, 134
Tocqueville, Alexis de, 71–72, 87
Tower, Senator John, 64
Tunney, Senator John V., 109–110

United Nations, 73, 87

Vinci, Leonardo da, 58
Verrocchio, 58
von Balthasar, Hans Urs, 40

141

Weber, Max, 44–45
Wilson, Edward O., 21
Wilson, Harold, 127
Wittgenstein's Vienna, 58

Yale University, 85

Zumwalt, Admiral Elmo, 62